Tuition Tax Credits
for Private Education

AN ECONOMIC ANALYSIS

Tuition Tax Credits
for Private Education

AN ECONOMIC ANALYSIS

Donald E. Frey
DEPARTMENT OF ECONOMICS
WAKE FOREST UNIVERSITY

Iowa State University Press / Ames, Iowa

© 1983 The Iowa State University Press
All rights reserved

Printed by The Iowa State University Press, Ames, Iowa 50010

First edition, 1983

Library of Congress Cataloging in Publication Data

Frey, Donald E., 1941–
   Tuition tax credits for private education.

   1. Tuition tax credits—United States.   I. Title.
HJ4653.C73F73   1983   336.24′216   83–12676
ISBN 0–8138–1826–5

The text in this book was printed from camera-ready copy supplied by the author.

CONTENTS

PREFACE

While this book was being prepared, the constitutionality of government aid to private education, including the tuition tax credit, remained an open issue. Indeed, the constitutional debate often obscured the fact that such aid raises equally important economic issues. Then, on June 29, 1983, the Supreme Court upheld the constitutionality of a Minnesota tax deduction for educational expenses, including private-school tuition. Legal scholars may argue whether or not this decision reversed the Court's previous position--in substance if not in form. However, the constitutional issue now is resolved. This resolution means that the public debate will shift to the wisdom, rather than the constitutionality, of government aid to private education. This book is a contribution to that debate.

Published Congressional hearings on tax subsidization of private education demonstrate that (1) important issues besides the constitutional issue exist, and (2) Congress has received almost no serious guidance on these issues. This book formulates several of these issues, suggests a theoretical framework in which answers can be found, and outlines some of the answers. The issues addressed are (1) the federal revenue loss from a tuition tax credit, (2) the possible increase of racial concentration and segregation in the schools, and (3) the possible loss of voter support for public schools. The tuition tax credit is analyzed because it is the form of subsidy to private education that clearly has the strongest support among lawmakers.

Chapter 1 provides a general overview of the private-

education sector and of the historic and legal background
of tax credits for private education.

Chapter 2 presents two econometric studies of the
market for private education. These studies are the
foundation for the remainder of the book. The noneconomist may find chapter 2 too technical and decide to move
to chapter 3; yet chapter 2 may be of considerable interest to applied economists or other technical analysts of
education policies, for no complete set of demand and
supply functions for private education have previously
been reported.

Estimates of federal revenue losses that would accompany a variety of tax credit plans are presented in
chapter 3. The analyses of chapter 3, which allow for
the adjustments of the private-education market to a tax
credit, suggest federal revenue losses to far exceed the
losses estimated by government analysts. A number of related issues are also considered.

Chapter 4 deals with the effect of a tax credit on
racial concentration and segregation in the education
systems of cities. The phenomenon of enrollment switching
from public to private schools, which would be induced by
a tax credit, is closely examined in this chapter; the
conclusion is that a tax credit would probably result in
public schools experiencing an increase in the proportion
of minority students in attendance. Evidence also suggests that this increased minority proportion would be
accompanied by some increase of segregation within the
public schools. However, both these effects appear to be
small for the kinds of tax credits contemplated.

Chapter 5 examines the possibility that tax breaks
for private tuition might reduce the number of parents
with a stake in the public schools, and that support for
public-education expenditures might thereby be reduced.
Some simple, theoretical reasoning and a review of a
number of studies reveals that it is not possible at present to conclude that higher enrollment in private schools
necessarily results in reduced voter support for public-
school expenditures.

In chapter 6 attention moves from the social costs of
a tax credit (lost tax revenue, increased segregation, or
the erosion of voter support for public education) to the
potential social benefits. For the benefit categories
considered, it is found that the tax credit is a very inefficient instrument for delivering funds to the intended

recipients; often several dollars of revenue loss occur
for every dollar actually reaching a member of a beneficiary category.

In chapter 7 an effort is made to anticipate any
major structural changes in the educational system that
would so alter things as to invalidate the analyses of
the book. Two significant eventualities considered are
(1) a massive collapse of confidence in public education
and (2) a major shift of private enrollment from the
North to the South. Consequences of these eventualities
are considered, but it is concluded that their occurrence
is remote. The chapter concludes with an assessment of
the political environment for tax credit legislation.

Both the method of analysis and the results of analysis are presented throughout. The discussion of method
includes theoretical models, data sources, formulas, statistical techniques, and so on; the discussion of results
includes concrete estimates of the impacts of the specific
tax credits under consideration. Specific estimates of
credit impacts are usually based on assumed values of
certain parameters or variables that are supported by
existing data. Using the formulas provided, the reader
is able to compute alternative estimates using other
parameter or variable values.

I am indebted to Wake Forest University for a
Reynolds research leave during the fall of 1981 when the
statistical work for this book was done. Additional small
grants from the Wake Forest Graduate Council's Research
and Publication Fund have facilitated typing and the ac-
quisition of data sources. Otherwise, this volume is the
product of independent research.

Portions of chapter 3 appeared originally as "The
Cost of a Tuition Tax Credit Reconsidered in the Light
of New Evidence," *Journal of Education Finance* 7(4)
450-461; reprinted by permission.

For the figures, I thank J. Van Wagstaff, colleague
and draftsman. The expert and exceedingly careful editing
of the Iowa State University Press staff is acknowledged
with gratitude.

Tuition Tax Credits
for Private Education

AN ECONOMIC ANALYSIS

CHAPTER 1

Overview

Political pressure for federal tax subsidization favoring private elementary and secondary education has been substantial in recent years. This chapter briefly discusses private education and governmental efforts for its assistance; the remainder of the book provides technical analyses of several possible outcomes of proposed tuition tax credits for private education.

PERSPECTIVE ON POLICY ANALYSIS

The tuition tax credit is an economic device that lowers the price of private schooling; thus it lends itself to economic analysis. Technical analysis of proposed policy changes prior to possible enactment by the U.S. Congress serves several important functions. To the degree that the rhetoric surrounding a policy proposal is unrealistic, policy analysis can redirect the rhetoric, clarify the legislature's intent, and give the courts better guidance in resolving subsequent litigation. Policy analysis may discover, before the fact, possible unintended effects and may permit modifications to minimize such effects. If modifications are not possible, policies discovered to have faults might be abandoned.

To be useful, ex ante policy analysis must provide estimates of the magnitudes of changes that are likely to be induced by a policy.[1] Quantitative estimates of policy effects require statistical analysis of past behavioral relations in order to make projections of future trends, even though past statistical relationships might not hold exactly in the future.[2] The exact data needed to estimate these behavioral relationships often do not exist. In

this event, the analyst may use proxies for the missing
data or may resort to simulations based on assumptions
about the nature of key relationships. Such assumptions
may or may not be buttressed with indirect evidence or
arguments.

These warnings about data need not negate the value
of ex ante quantitative policy analysis. If an estimated
range of projections is acceptable the analyst can specify
alternative assumptions from which a range of effects of a
proposed policy can be deduced, with the most likely outcome almost certainly to be found within the range. Even
if such an approach specifies only the order of magnitude
of an effect, it is often superior to a nonquantitative
approach.

In keeping with this perspective, the analysis of
the tuition tax credit presented in subsequent chapters
provides quantitative estimates of effects that the
credit may have. The reader is informed of the kinds of
statistical data, relationships, and assumptions that
underlie the estimates.

DEFINITIONS AND DISTINCTIONS
The large number of programs of federal aid to
higher education demonstrates the abundance of methods
whereby aid can be channeled to private elementary and
secondary schools.[3] Yet efforts in recent years to provide federal aid to private schools have concentrated
heavily on forms of tax relief to the exclusion of other
devices. This approach is apparently dictated by the
hope that tax relief may be more capable of passing the
test of constitutionality than other kinds of aid.

A tuition tax *deduction* would allow a taxpayer to
deduct all or some portion of tuition payments from gross
income before figuring the amount of tax owed. This
method bestows larger benefits on taxpayers in higher tax
brackets than on lower income private school users. Like
medical care deductions, a tuition tax deduction could be
restricted to tuition expenses that exceed some given percent of one's gross income; other kinds of restrictions
could be devised. In general, such restrictions would
serve to direct tax relief toward or away from particular
categories of private-school users.

As perceived by advocates of aid to private schools,
the tax deduction for tuition has the major problem that

one must itemize deductions in order to benefit. Some
users of nonpublic schools, such as low-income families
enrolling students in urban parochial schools, may fail
to benefit, because they rarely itemize. As the standard
tax deduction has risen over the years, numerous middle-
class families have ceased to itemize deductions.

The tuition tax *credit* is free of these problems.
The credit allows one to reduce the amount of tax owed
(not merely the income on which the tax is figured) by an
amount equal to some portion of tuition paid to private
schools. Under this approach the benefit would be equal
for people paying equal amounts of tuition, whatever
their bracket or whether they itemize deductions. The
credit could be made "refundable" so that persons with
incomes too low to owe any tax at all would receive a
payment from the government equal to the credit.

The distinction between credit and deduction is
not merely academic. Private schools whose client families are of moderate income (e.g., urban parochial
schools) should prefer the credit to the deduction,
while schools whose client families are of higher income
(e.g., independent "prep" schools) may have a preference
for the deduction.

Independent and parochial schools may also have
conflicting interests as to the form of the credit itself.
Suppose Congress enacted a tax credit for tuition, but
decided to limit the revenue loss to the Treasury. This
could be accomplished in two ways: (1) the proportion of
tuition that one is allowed to claim as a credit may be
reduced or (2) a limit to the amount of credit that any
one taxpayer may claim in a year could be set. If they
were forced to choose between such alternatives, schools
charging relatively low tuition should favor a credit
plan with high percentages and low limits, while high-
tuition schools should prefer lower percentages with
high limits. The logic of this is illustrated in
Table 1.1, where plans A and B may be assumed to provide
an equal revenue loss to the U.S. Treasury. Parents
using the high-tuition school find plan A more profitable,
while parents using the low-tuition school find plan B

Table 1.1. Benefits Received by Low- and High-Tuition Taxpayers

Tuition	Plan A 25% of Tuition to $1000	Plan B 70% of Tuition to $300
$3000	$750	$300
400	100	280

more profitable. In general, the design of a plan for
a tax credit is not a matter of indifference to the
potential beneficiaries.

Tax *deferrals* would permit a taxpayer to defer
paying a portion of tax owed equal to some proportion
of tuition paid to private schools. The deferral is
actually a loan, which raises issues in addition to those
already considered; for example, what is the appropriate
interest rate, and how fast should the payback be? Since
the government would hope eventually to recoup the de-
ferred amounts, Congress may be less inclined to place
low limits on the amount of deferrals allowed. In this
respect, the deferral differs from the credit and deduction, both of which would produce permanent losses to the
Treasury.

EXAMPLE OF PROPOSED LEGISLATION

Senate bill S.550 of 1981 is broadly representative
of past proposals for the tuition tax credit, and it is
likely that a tax credit that Congress might pass would
resemble this bill. Bill S.550 would allow a refundable
credit of 50 percent of educational expenses up to a
maximum of $250 for the first year and $500 each year
thereafter.[4] It would initially apply to students from
the first grade through undergraduate college and eventually include graduate students. The bill defines eligible elementary and secondary schools as those privately
operated on a nonprofit basis, as "nonprofit" is defined
by the Internal Revenue Service (IRS). To be eligible,
schools may not exclude students because of race, color,
or national/ethnic origin, although exclusion on grounds
of religion is permitted.[5] Bill S.550 also omits any
standards for teacher certification, pupil-teacher ratios,
library or other facilities, accreditation, or student
performance, nor does it require or permit any federal
agency to establish such standards for a school to be
eligible for the tax credit. (The reason has to do with
the constitutional requirement of separation of church
and state.) A number of additional provisions deal with
such issues as the kinds of educational expenses (e.g.,
book purchases, meals on campus) that are not eligible
for the credit, the relation of the credit to other kinds
of federal grants to recipients, and court procedures to
be followed if parts of the law are challenged.

Bill S.550 also contains a statement of policy that

actually enumerates several diverse goals. The primary purpose of the credit is "to enhance equality of educational opportunity . . ." It also is federal policy to foster "educational choice" and to recognize the "right of parents to direct the education and upbringing of their children." Finally, Congress "finds, without [the tuition tax credit] the personal liberty, diversity, and pluralism which constitute important strengths of education would be diminished . . ." The declaration of policy does not consider whether these goals are themselves compatible with each other.

STATISTICAL PORTRAIT OF PRIVATE EDUCATION
        With the exception of certain surveys by the National Catholic Educational Association, no systematic gathering of data on the private sector occurs on a regular basis. Surveys have been conducted irregularly for a variety of purposes; indirect evidence may be gleaned from other sources such as the decennial census or the Current Population Survey (CPS) conducted in October of each year. These surveys are of limited value because they always survey households, not the schools themselves, thus restricting the kinds of questions that can be asked. Households are asked if any of their children attend private schools and even what tuition is paid (asked only in 1978 and 1979); this information can be cross-tabulated with the household's income, race, or geographical location, creating a statistical portrait of the kinds of people using the nonpublic schools. However, such surveys provide no information about the kinds of nonpublic schools attended.
        A recent universal survey of private schools was the three-year survey of approximately twenty thousand identified private schools from 1976-1977 to 1978-1979, funded by the National Center for Education Statistics. The survey was limited in scope, concentrating on size of staff, enrollment, curriculum type, and revenue sources; but it omitted questions dealing with racial composition of the student population, student performance, teacher certification, and related issues that might be considered controversial. About 10 percent of the known schools did not respond, even after repeated contacts, perhaps revealing a suspicion of government. In addition to those that did not respond, some private schools may never have been identified at all. This

8 CHAPTER 1

Table 1.2. Summary of Private School Statistics

	1932-33	1940-41	1960-61	1970-71	1978-79
Schools	10,315	12,727	18,374	17,569	19,663
Enrollment	2,026,625	2,611,047	5,236,480	5,143,182	5,084,297
Teachers	68,307	94,977	182,170	216,824	272,664
Average number					
pupils per school	196	205	312	292	259
pupils per teacher	29.7	27.5	28.7	23.7	18.6
elementary	35.8	33.2	37.5	26.9	22.5
secondary	14.1	15.2	18.8	17.3	17.1
teachers per school	6.6	7.5	9.9	12.3	13.9
Church-affiliated schools, %	89.4	91.3	90.2	83.6	79.9
Private enrollment, %	7.7	10.4	13.6	10.1	10.7

Source: Roy C. Nehrt, *Private Schools in American Education* (Washington, D.C.: Nat. Center Ed. Stat., 1981), Table A.

preface on the quality of the data should cause the reader to appreciate the somewhat tentative nature of the portrait presented here.

The high-water mark of private elementary and secondary attendance occurred around 1960 (Table 1.2), though intradecade data probably would show that the peak occurred somewhat later in the sixties. This peak of 13.6 percent of school students in private schools seems in retrospect to have been an aberration rather than the culmination of a normal trend, for both before and after 1960 the proportion of students in private schools was approximately 10 percent. Nevertheless, by 1970-1971, private enrollment had dropped about 100,000 from the 1960 figure, even while public enrollments were increasing strongly. The decline was actually concentrated in the latter years of the decade, and many enrollment projections based on trends established in the late 1960s were gloomy indeed.[6]

Table 1.2 reveals other important patterns. On average, private schools are small and have been so over the 50 years covered by the table. The peak average enrollment in 1960-1961 probably represented some crowding; in recent years average enrollment has dropped. The number of teachers per school rose throughout the era shown and, coupled with the pupil enrollment pattern, resulted in a dramatic reduction in the average pupil-teacher ratio. Finally, the data in Table 1.2 demonstrates the crux of much debate over the constitutionality of governmental assistance to private schools; even in the most recent year shown, church-affiliated schools accounted for about 80 percent of all nonpublic elementary and secondary schools.

Several features stand out in the pattern of expenditures in the nonpublic sector for two recent years (Table 1.3). The nonaffiliated private schools spend substantially more per pupil than the church-affiliated

Table 1.3. Current Expenditure per Pupil in Private School by Affiliation and Type

| Type of School | Total | Church-Affiliated | | | Nonaffiliated |
		Catholic	Lutheran	Other	
Elementary					
1976-77	460	394	543	653	960
1977-78	512	438	579	908	870
Secondary					
1976-77	1092	796	1195	2105	2953
1977-78	1165	853	1097	2287	3163
Combined					
1976-77	1145	746	654	882	1500
1977-78	1195	777	637	795	1710
Other					
1976-77	2811	2268	3798	1756	3030
1977-78	2939	2256	2294	2191	3158
Total					
1976-77	760	514	628	935	1704
1977-78	819	561	651	981	1822

Source: *Selected Public and Private Elementary and Secondary Education Statistics: School Years 1976-77 through 1978-79,* NCES Bull. 80-B01 (Washington, D.C.: Nat. Center Ed. Stat., 1979), Table 13.

schools. As might be expected, secondary school expenditures are much higher than elementary expenditures. The high-spending "other" schools include schools providing special education or vocational education. Comparing the costs of the private schools, which are highly concentrated in the Northeast, with a typical public school there would reveal that public expenditures are comparable to those of the nonaffiliated private schools but higher, by a substantial margin, than the church-affiliated schools. Although a comparable breakdown is not available for all private schools, tuition covers only about 40 percent of costs in Roman Catholic elementary schools and about 75 percent in Catholic secondary schools (Table 1.4). The substantial parish subsidies received by parochial elementary schools prove of importance for the analysis of the link between enrollment and costs of attending private schools. Table 1.4 does not show the value of services contributed by teachers who are members of religious orders and who receive only small stipends.

Table 1.4. Sources of per Pupil Revenue for Roman Catholic Schools: 1978-79

	Elementary (%)	Secondary (%)
Tuition and fees	39.6	77.1
Parish subsidy	49.5)	10.2
Diocesan subsidy	1.5)	
Fund raising/other	9.4	12.7

Sources: *Catholic Elementary Schools and Their Finances* (Washington, D.C.: Nat. Catholic Ed. Assoc., 1980), Table 8; *Catholic High Schools and Their Finances* (Washington, D.C.: Nat. Catholic Ed. Assoc., 1980), Table 5 (restated to reflect categories used by elementary schools).

POLITICAL HISTORY

Tax credits for higher education have been proposed since 1967, although the House of Representatives did not

approve such a bill until 1978. In 1972, both candidates
for president endorsed the concept of tax relief for educational expenses, including elementary and secondary
expenditures. In this, they followed a presidential commission's 1972 recommendation that nonpublic schools receive all "constitutionally permissible" aid and "additional and more substantive forms of assistance e.g.,
(1) tax credits."[7] The rhetoric of support for this
plan in the early 1970s tended to emphasize the plight
of the private schools (tight finances and declining :
enrollments) and the cost to the public of "absorbing"
displaced private-school students. In 1972, however,
the bill did not pass.

Tuition tax credits reappeared in the form of the
Roth amendment to the Social Security Financing Amend-
ments of 1977. The impact of the Social Security re-
visions of 1977 was felt most keenly by members of the
upper middle class (since the wage base on which Social
Security taxes would be collected was increased substantially at that time). In view of the significant outcry
raised by professional and managerial taxpayers, the Roth
proposal was for a tuition tax credit for higher education as a form of "middle-class tax relief," the premise
being that college costs were a significant burden to the
upper-middle class. Although the Roth amendment was not
adopted, the apparent popularity of tuition tax credits
paved the way for the near success in 1978 of credit
legislation championed most strongly by Senators Robert
Packwood and Daniel Moynihan, and Congressman Charles
Vanik. Unlike the 1977 Roth proposal, the 1978 bills
represented clear attempts to provide credits for elementary and secondary tuition.

By 1978 the House of Representatives, which had
previously opposed tax relief for private elementary and
secondary schools, had definitely changed its mind. However, now the administration opposed the concept. The
Jimmy Carter administration proposed extremely generous
increases in existing grant and loan programs for college
students, apparently hoping to divide those favoring
credits for college from those favoring them for elementary and secondary schooling. The progress of the
credit through Congress was confused, and it was not
clear at the time that the Carter strategy to stop the
tax credit would be successful.[8] In the end, however,
the Senate refused to accept a compromise version of a

tax credit bill that called for elementary and secondary credit.

The opposition of the Carter administration to credits may be linked to at least three factors: (1) support of the president by public school teachers' unions, (2) adherence to traditional Democratic party programs for public education, and (3) the president's personal Baptist views that traditionally favor strict separation of church and state. The Reagan presidency is influenced by none of these. Besides having no constituency in the teachers' unions and having no obligation to Democratic programs, the Reagan candidacy was committed to private-sector answers to problems, including those of education; and support for the Reagan candidacy was from religious organizations that do not share as strong a commitment to church and state separation as the traditional Baptist view of Carter.

Despite the April 1982 proposal of a tuition tax credit by the Reagan administration, a growing concern for federal budget deficits, increased by the tax cuts of 1981, prevented passage of a credit in 1982. In 1983 the Ronald Reagan administration introduced another credit proposal designed to add as little as possible to the large federal deficit. The object now seems to be to pass a very small credit that would establish credits in principle while postponing increases until a more prosperous day.

LEGAL STATUS

To the extent that the Supreme Court's interpretation of the constitutionality of state aid to church-affiliated schools has crystallized in the last decade, the cause of tuition tax credits, along with other aid, would seem to be in jeopardy. Several kinds of aid to private schools, several of which closely resemble the proposed federal tuition tax credit, have been declared unconstitutional under the establishment clause of the First Amendment. By 1971 the Court had developed a three-part test to determine if laws extending state aid to private schools are constitutional under the First Amendment: (1) the law must have a secular purpose; (2) the primary effect of the law must neither advance nor inhibit religion; (3) the law must avoid excessive entanglement of government with religion.

An unconstitutional "entanglement" may occur if state
funding leads religious groups to lobby and campaign
annually for increased funding. Entanglement may also
occur if government attempts to regulate church schools
because they must be accountable for their use of state
funds. A few kinds of aid to nonpublic education had
been permitted prior to the development of the three-
part test, and these continue to be permitted.

Despite the exceptions, the three-part test, as
applied since *Committee for Public Education and
Religious Liberty et al.* v *Nyquist et al.* (1973), has
generally resulted in the finding that state plans of
aid for private schools are unconstitutional. In the
Nyquist case, the Court found that a New York state law
that provided tax relief for tuition at private schools
was unconstitutional for failing the second part of the
three-part test. This case has been followed by a
series of other decisions finding various kinds of state
tax relief to parochial schools to be unconstitutional.[9]

Advocates of a federal tuition tax credit nevertheless persist in the hope that a federal credit would not
meet the fate of state programs. One line of thought
points out that the Court has approved some kinds of
state aid to sectarian higher education. Noting that
the distinction between higher education and secondary,
or even elementary, education is to some degree arbitrary,
advocates of the credit hold that the Court may someday
be convinced that it has been inconsistent in holding to
two standards--one for higher and one for elementary and
secondary education.

Another approach is to meet the three-part test
head-on and to build safeguards against all three of the
hazards into a federal credit. The "secular purpose"
test is easily met simply by stating a secular purpose,
because the Court has been inclined to accept at face
value the stated purposes of legislatures in passing
laws. While it may be impossible to prevent a tax
credit from aiding religion in some degree, it may be
possible to design the credit so that aid to religion
would be an incidental effect of the credit, not its
primary effect.[10] Finally, the entanglement test might
be passed by requiring that the government set virtually
no standards for the private schools that benefit from
the tax credit; if there are no standards that the
sectarian schools must meet on grounds of accountability,

any possible entanglement associated with the government's policing its standards can be avoided.[11]

An approach used by Christian fundamentalists is the claim that public schools cannot be neutral in matters of religion. In this view, the failure of public schools to endorse (or at least give equal time to) fundamentalist positions is equated not with neutrality but with hostility to their faith. From this for-us-or-against-us perspective, the failure of the state to subsidize sectarian schools is to impose hostile religious beliefs in the public schools; this, of course, would not be constitutional.[12] Because past decisions of the Supreme Court seem to be predicated on the belief that neutrality in matters of religion is possible, the Court would appear unlikely to accept this argument unless it is willing to make a complete break with past decisions.

A last ground for hope that the Court might approve of tax credits lies also in a fundamental reinterpretation of long-held views, in this case of the establishment clause of the First Amendment. As expounded by advocates of aid to private schools, the meaning of the clause that Congress "shall make no law respecting an establishment of religion" is that the government is forbidden from preferential treatment of *one* denomination but not from evenhanded distribution of benefits to all denominations. This argument hangs by the article an, and it is puzzling that the First Amendment was not worded in a manner to make this interpretation rely on less tenuous support if this interpretation had been intended.[13] This interpretation has in the past not been accepted by the Court.

WHAT CREDIT PROPOSALS SEEK TO DO

The tuition tax credit described by bill S.550 of 1981, with which the reader is already familiar in some detail, outlines a number of purposes or goals: the enhancement of equality of educational opportunity, educational diversity, personal liberty and choice, and parental rights to direct children's education. The meanings of these terms are not defined in the bill itself. In addition, various proponents of tuition tax credits have also cited goals of middle-class tax relief, avoidance of the necessity of public schools absorbing displaced students when private schools fail, allowing inner-city children to afford private educations, and

alleviating a perceived double taxation when one pays
both education taxes and private-school tuition.

The diversity of stated goals suggests that support
for tuition tax credits depends on a coalition of groups
with somewhat different interests. The effort to direct
the credit at a single goal would presumably weaken its
support among some groups. For example, if the single
goal of the tuition tax credit were to help low-income,
inner-city children attend private schools, the bill
might be limited to families with incomes below a certain
level; by excluding higher income families, all the benefits of the credit could then be concentrated on low-
income children. However, in order to obtain the support
of middle- and upper-income families, bill S.550 is not
written in that way. The result is that the bill obtains
wider political support but becomes far more expensive
than if it were focused on a single goal. In short, the
tax credits proposed as legislation have tended to set
out to achieve a number of sometimes related, sometimes
unrelated, goals. The immediate result of this has been
to build political support for credit plans, but the
ultimate result has been that the bills lack a clear
focus.

Whatever the stated goals of proponents of the
tuition tax credit, opponents have cited a number of
possible outcomes that are usually considered unde-
sirable: high costs of a tuition tax credit (interpreted
either as lost federal revenue or as costs inflicted on
other federal policies), the constitutional issues discussed earlier, the impact of the credit on the integration of public school systems, and the undermining of
local support for public schools. Several of these
issues are analyzed fully in chapters 3-5, following an
econometric study of the market for private education in
chapter 2.

NOTES

1. Without some estimate of the magnitude of
changes, the theoretical elaboration of likely changes
would be of minor importance; even changes that are very
bad in a qualitative sense may be tolerable if they are
small in magnitude and short in duration. Some economists
who have written on educational policy, however, have
advanced and defended proposals on almost purely theo-

retical grounds; this represents a judgment that some
outcomes are desirable on philosophical grounds, no
matter if the size of the outcome is small or large.
Milton Friedman, *Capitalism and Freedom* (Chicago: Univ.
Chicago Press, 1962), 85–107.

 2. For example, examine the projections of Roman
Catholic enrollments for the year 1980 by Kenneth M.
Brown in *Economic Problems of Nonpublic Schools: A
Report to the President's Commission on School Finance,*
ed. F. J. Fahey (Notre Dame, Ind.: Notre Dame Univ.,
1972). Projections for 1980 enrollments were 1.4 million
(elementary) and 0.69 million (secondary); actual enrollments were 2.3 million and 0.84 million, respectively.

 3. Federal aid directed to college students or
their parents has included federal grants; fellowships
and scholarships; subsidized loans; work-study programs;
benefits for students under veterans' and social
security survivors' laws; exemptions for dependent students on parents' income tax; and tax-free status of
fellowships, scholarships, and related benefits. Federal
aid directed to institutions themselves has included
grants for curriculum development, faculty improvement,
or equipment purchases; subsidization of some kinds of
campus facilities; payments for some types of students,
such as medical students; provision of faculty for
military-related parts of the curriculum; nonprofit
status for income tax purposes. Significantly, federal
aid to higher education does not include tax relief
related to the amount spent on tuition or fees.

 4. The tuition tax credit proposed by the Reagan
administration in April 1982 provided (like S.550), a
50 percent credit up to $500. The credit was not refund-
able and was to be phased out for taxpayers with incomes
between $50,000 and $70,000. The 1983 proposal of the
administration replaces the $500 cap with a $300 cap and
phases out the credit between $40,000 and $60,000.

 5. The bill does not itself define what constitutes discriminatory exclusion, apparently leaving
enforcement to the IRS, which in the past has been
prevented by congressional criticism from developing
rigorous standards.

 6. During the late 1960s and early 1970s, the
effort to obtain federal assistance for parochial schools
was predicated on the view that without financial assistance the private sector might fail altogether, forcing
the public schools to absorb millions of pupils. Even

scholars who seemed cool to the idea of federal assistance to private schools dealt extensively with the cost
of "absorbing" pupils from the closing private schools
into the public schools. Daniel Sullivan, *Public Aid to
Nonpublic Schools* (Lexington, Mass.: Heath, 1974),
Appendix 4-B. By the mid-1970s it was evident that the
situation had stabilized, and Table 1.2 shows that by
1978 private enrollment had returned to 10.7 percent of
total enrollment. (This stabilization of enrollment
masked the fact that within the private sector Roman
Catholic schools continued to lose enrollment while
other nonpublic schools gained.)

7. President's Commission on School Finance,
Final Report: Schools, People, and Money (Washington,
D.C.: USGPO, 1972), xvi. The commission also linked
the proposal of aid for private schools with a condition
that they be accountable to the public to provide information on enrollment, finances, performance, etc.

8. This confusion is seen in the fact that the
House Ways and Means Committee, during its April markup
sessions on the credit bill, twice reversed itself on
fundamental points. In the end the full House insisted
on elementary and secondary tax credits, while the full
Senate refused. Though they agreed on college credits,
the deadlock on a compromise bill persisted when Congress
adjourned shortly before the election.

9. In May 1979 the Court upheld without comment a
lower federal court's decision invalidating a New Jersey
tax deduction for dependents attending private schools.

10. For example, churches keep their local property
tax exemptions in part because they receive the exemption
as members of a far broader category of beneficiaries--
nonprofit organizations. If the credit were broadly
written so as to include colleges, universities, and
even public elementary and secondary schools, the aid
to the sectarian schools might be interpreted as only
incidental.

11. This makes the problem of accountability most
acute. Federal funds would benefit schools that cannot
be held accountable to federal or state standards lest
the policing of the standards lead to unconstitutional
entanglement. See Donald E. Frey, "The Tuition Tax
Credit: Uncertain Directions in Public Policy," in
Family Choice in Schooling, ed. M. Manley-Casimir
(Lexington, Mass.: Heath, 1982).

12.   Martin E. Marty, "We're No Holier for Our 'Holy War'," *New York Times* (22 July 1981), for a short history of the development of this position.

13.   A study favorable to this reinterpretation is Michael Malbin, *Religion and Politics: The Intentions of the Authors of the First Amendment* (Washington, D.C.: Am. Ent. Inst., 1978).

C H A P T E R   2

Demand and Supply Functions for Private Education

A tuition tax credit would reduce the net payments by parents for private schooling, thereby increasing the demand. Such an increase in demand, under a range of realistic conditions, would induce increases in tuition rates, increases in private enrollment, reductions in public-school enrollment, and losses in federal revenue. If statistical estimates of the demand and supply functions for private education existed, one could estimate the size of these predicted effects; lacking this knowledge, one could not forecast even the general magnitude of increases in tuition and enrollment that might occur. Yet, almost no estimates of demand functions, and no estimates of supply functions for private education exist.[1] This chapter presents four empirical studies of demand and supply for private education, thereby filling this gap.

This chapter reports in some detail the methods, data sources, and results of a research project that estimated the demand and supply elasticities of the private sector in education; these estimates form the basis for most subsequent chapters. The reader whose interest is mainly in policy results and who is willing to accept the statistical estimates at face value may wish to move to chapter 3, in which mathematical and diagrammatic models illustrate how a tuition tax credit may shift the equilibrium existing between demand and supply functions for private education and result in changed enrollment and tuition levels. The degree of these changes depends on the degree of responsiveness (elasticities) of enrollment demand or supply to changes in tuition. We turn now to the task of estimating these elasticities.

MODELS OF THE PRIVATE SCHOOL MARKET

Prior to seeing the statistical evidence, one might think that any of three possible models might best describe the structure of the market for private education. An *equilibrium model* E incorporates conventional market-clearing assumptions:

$$E_S = bT + gS \qquad \text{(supply equation)} \qquad (2.1)$$

$$E_D = -aT + hD \qquad \text{(demand equation)} \qquad (2.2)$$

$$E_D = E_S \qquad \text{(equilibrium condition)} \qquad (2.3)$$

where E_D and E_S are enrollment demand and supply, T is tuition, S and D are vectors of exogenous supply and demand variables, and the lowercase letters are coefficients. Equations (2.1)–(2.3) permit the estimation of both demand and supply functions using conventional regression techniques that allow for simultaneity in endogenous variables.

What might be called a *quasi-equilibrium model* EQ would allow for private schools to engage in a selective admissions process (i.e., rationing of places) but would retain the joint determination of tuition and enrollment in a model composed of (2.1), (2.2), and

$$E_S = mE_D \qquad (2.4)$$

where m is a constant less than one in value. Equation (2.4) requires that the number of places supplied by private schools only be a proportion of demand. Equations (2.1), (2.2), and (2.4) produce determinate values for tuition and enrollment despite the presence of nonprice rationing, which means that the number of applicants E_D exceeds the number of places E_S. If model EQ is the proper representation of the market for private schooling, the supply function and a quasi-demand function,

$$mE_D = -amT + hmD \qquad (2.5)$$

can be estimated using actual observations on enrollment and tuition.[2] Yet, for the purpose of assessing the impact of a tuition tax credit, estimates of (2.5) are sufficient; even if it is possible to estimate only am rather than a alone, the estimate of the enrollment

elasticity of demand with respect to tuition will be the
same.   That is, while there may be no way to distinguish
model E from EQ if there is insufficient information to
estimate the value of m, policy estimates of the impact
of a tuition tax credit will be the same.

It is possible, however, to specify a *rationing
model* R where nonprice rationing is less systematic than
in model EQ.   Consider a model of the market for private
schooling consisting of (2.1) and

$$T = \overline{T} < T*$$

where $\overline{T}$ is the level of tuition specified exogenously by
the private schools and is less than the market-clearing
tuition T*.   Here, enrollment is determined by the supply
function, and a demand function cannot be estimated from
observed enrollment and tuition data.   Model R is a true
rationing model.

Without data on applications (versus enrollment)
for private schools, models E and EQ cannot be distinguished econometrically from one another, but the two
can be distinguished from R.   The former models imply
that both supply and demand (or quasi-demand) functions
can be estimated; the latter implies that only the supply
function can be estimated.   The former, in addition,
imply that tuition and enrollment are simultaneously
determined, while the latter makes tuition an exogenous
variable.   If models E or EQ hold, ordinary least squares
estimates of the coefficients of tuition should contain a
positive bias term for demand and a negative bias term
for supply.[3]

The demand vector D contains a number of control
variables.   We postulate first that preference for nonpublic education is determined to a high degree by religious affiliation (i.e., the probability that children
will attend private schools varies by denominational
affiliation).   The historic fact that some denominations
perceive public schools to be promulgating insufficient
or wrong values lies behind this hypothesis.   We hypothe-
size also that if private education is a normal good, enrollment per capita should be related directly to measures
of income.   Theory also suggests that price and quality of
substitutes for private education have a bearing on demand.   Although the major substitute, public education,
is not priced for users, the quality of public education
should be inversely related to the demand for private

education. Unfortunately, measures of public-school
quality (e.g., expenditure per pupil) are too highly
correlated with other income indicators to obtain plausible results for the impact of public-school quality on
the demand for private education. The issue of public-
school quality does, however, suggest a subsidiary hypothesis. If this quality difference is actually less in
high-income communities, public schools are a better substitute for private schools there than in low-income
communities. An interaction variable (tuition multiplied
by an income variable) is included in the regressions to
test the hypothesis that poorer substitutes for private
schools exist in low-income than in high-income markets.

Specifying the supply vector S requires that one
take account of the nonprofit nature of private education, which may rule out a conventional supply function
for the individual school. Freeman argues for a supply
function defined as the average cost function for values
of tuition above the point where the schools would lose
money on their operations and the marginal cost function
below that point.[4] Unlike the for-profit firm, the
school may obtain revenues in the form of donations, so
the cost curves defined in terms of the unsubsidized
portion of costs vary with the amount of donations. The
costs of operation determine the supply function for
private education and these are, in turn, greatly
determined by input prices. Because of the high degree
of church affiliation of private schools, the cost of
staff is highly influenced by the degree to which facul-
ties are members of religious orders who typically work
for only subsistence. The costs may also be affected by
scale economies or diseconomies. Scale economies in education are typically exhausted by relatively small
schools; private schools tend to be in this range.[5] A
final hypothesis is that regulations regarding pupil-
teacher ratios, kinds of equipment, accreditation, etc.,
affect the costs of private education. The specific
proxy variables needed to test these hypotheses are
considered below.

Alternative Definitions of Tuition

A tuition variable is common to both demand and
supply equations and is determined jointly with enrollment if model E or EQ holds. The proper definition of
tuition, however, requires discussion. The data on pri-

vate schools used in this study report certain revenues
as "tuition and fee" revenues. This tuition and fee
revenue divided by enrollment is the most straightforward
definition of tuition that could be used; however Sullivan
reported that a broader definition of tuition performed
well in his studies of individual schools' demand functions.[6] To nominal tuition and fees per pupil was added
the per pupil amount of other reported school revenues to
define a broad tuition measure. The rationale is that
tax laws encourage schools to keep nominal tuition low
while requesting that parents make up the difference with
tax-deductible donations in lieu of tuition.[7] If this
practice is widespread, nominal tuition understates the
true charges paid by parents. In the research reported
below, two tuition definitions are tested where sufficient data are available.

EMPIRICAL METHODOLOGY
        Four market demand and four market supply studies,
utilizing two distinct data bases, were conducted. One
data base covered Roman Catholic elementary and secondary
schools during the two-year period 1968-1970; the other
covered all private elementary and secondary schools during the period 1976-1978. To the degree that the data
sources permitted, the same, or similar, variables were
utilized in the regressions. In all cases, both two-stage
least squares (TSLS) and ordinary least squares (OLS)
estimation techniques were used to test for evidence of
the simultaneous determination of enrollment and tuition.
The unit of observation has been the state; lack of data
on an annual basis for smaller areas, such as Standard
Metropolitan Statistical Areas (SMSAs) or cities, made
it impossible to define smaller market areas. Because
the use of states as observations tends to limit the
degrees of freedom, data in all cases were pooled over
two-year periods to increase the number of observations;
Chow tests were performed on several of the regressions
to assure that pooling of data was a legitimate procedure.
        The definitions of the variables and the data
sources, along with sample mean values of the variables,
are given in the appendix to this chapter. However, a
few points should be made here. The major obstacle to
an empirical study of the market for private education
is obtaining tuition and financial data for the private
sector because these data are not regularly published in

any source; conversely, enrollment data for private schools are relatively easy to obtain. The primary data source for both financial and enrollment variables for the 1976-1978 study was the National Center for Education Statistics (see appendix to this chapter). The data for individual schools were aggregated at the state level to obtain market-level data on enrollment, tuition revenue, nontuition revenue, and staffing. Elementary and secondary schools constituted separate samples, and no effort was made to include schools that did not fit clearly into the elementary or secondary category. A few variables, such as state per capita income levels were obtained from generally available public sources such as the U.S. Statistical Abstracts. For the 1968-1970 study of Catholic schools, there were two major data sources. Tuition revenue figures were obtained from the appendix to the report conducted by Notre Dame.[8] Enrollment and staffing data came from publications of the National Catholic Educational Association. These data, in general, were available only at the state level of aggregation.

The TSLS regression technique involved estimating tuition as a function of all exogenous demand and supply variables, including a number of regional dummy variables that could not be assigned a priori to either demand or supply status. After estimating both reduced-form tuition and enrollment equations, it was possible to assign the regional dummy variables to either the demand or supply category in each sample on the basis of the values of their coefficients in the reduced-form regressions. Regional dummy variables in the supply category were not included in structural demand regressions and vice versa; however, when the role of a regional variable was ambiguous--as when its coefficient was insignificant in one of the reduced-form regressions--it was assigned to both structural regressions rather than dropped. Those exogenous variables for which theoretical expectations exist were dropped only if the sign of their coefficient in the reduced-form tuition regression was opposite that expected; this occurred only rarely.

DEMAND EQUATIONS

Estimates of the structural demand equations for the private sector are given in Table 2.1. Parts A through D cover four distinct studies defined by school type and time period: all nonpublic elementary schools, 1976-1978;

Table 2.1. Demand for Nonpublic Education (dependent variable: proportion of age group enrolled)

Con-stant	D_1	D_2	D_3	T	I	R	Y	No.	R^2	Type	Regr.
A. Nonpublic elementary, 1976-78											
.02	.002* (6.7)	-.001* (3.8)	-.0007* (2.7)	-.00006* (4.0) [-0.34]				98	.658	OLS	2.1.1
.037	.002* (6.4)	.001* (4.0)	.001* (3.1)	-.00009* (3.7) [-0.50]				98	.649	TSLS	2.1.2
.06	.002* (6.1)	.002* (4.6)	-.002* (4.0)	-.00017* (4.3) [-0.37] [-0.16]a	.000003** (2.5)			98	.672	TSLS	2.1.3
.083	.001* (4.7)	.002* (5.1)	-.001* (3.5)	-.00016*b (4.7) [-1.4]				98	.674	TSLS	2.1.4
.13	.001* (5.1)	.002* (5.3)	-.003* (3.5)	-.00024*b (5.1) [-0.96] [-0.54]a	.000003 (2.4)			98	.694	TSLS	2.1.5
B. Catholic elementary, 1968-70											
-.022	.001* (4.5)	.003* (3.4)		-.00048* (2.9) [-0.23]		-.006 (0.7)		87	.514	OLS	2.1.6
-.001	.001* (4.1)	.003* (3.6)		-.001* (3.5) [-0.50]		-.006 (0.7)		87	.533	TSLS	2.1.7
-.49	.001* (4.3)	.019* (5.9)		.0098* (4.5) [+]a	-.0003* (5.0)	-.008 (1.1)		87	.644	TSLS	2.1.8
C. Nonpublic secondary, 1976-78											
.053				-.00002* (3.6) [-0.34]				100	.698	OLS	2.1.9
.06				-.00002* (3.4) [-0.41]				100	.693	TSLS	2.1.10
.029		.0005*** (1.7)		-.00002*b (2.9) [-0.44]				100	.729	TSLS	2.1.11
.031		.0004 (0.4)		-.000019b (0.4) [-0.43] [-0.43]a	-2×10^{-8} (.03)			100	.729	TSLS	2.1.12
D. Catholic secondary, 1968-70											
-.025	.002* (6.6)	.001** (2.3)		-.00004*** (1.8) [-0.14]				84	.770	OLS	2.1.13
-.051	.003* (8.8)	.006* (5.5)		-.0006* (5.1) [-2.1]				84	.822	TSLS	2.1.14
-.05	.003* (8.7)	.006* (3.3)		-.0006*** (2.4) [-2.1] [-2.1]a	1×10^{-7} (00)			84	.822	TSLS	2.1.15

Absolute t-values ( ); elasticities [ ].

Definitions of variables: D_1 = % of state population that is Roman Catholic; D_2 = state per capita income (in hundreds); D_3 = % of private schools with Title I program; T = mean tuition in private schools of state (nominal, unless otherwise indicated); I = interaction variable: T times D_3 in A; T times D_2 elsewhere; R = regional dummy variable(s), coefficients omitted; Y = year dummy, included only where significant in at least one regression.

Levels of significance: * significant at greater than 1%, two-side test; ** significant at greater than 5%, two-side test; *** significant at greater than 10%, two-side test.

    a. Elasticity calculated with D_3 set one standard deviation above mean or D_2 set

Catholic elementary, 1968–1970; all nonpublic secondary, 1976–1978; and Catholic secondary, 1968–1970, respectively. The results in the four parts are discussed sequentially. All regression coefficients except those for regional dummy variables, which are of no interest, are reported.

In part A, all coefficients for which hypotheses have been proposed have the expected signs, and all the coefficients have a high degree of statistical significance (greater than the 1 percent level). The percent of the population D_1 that is Roman Catholic has a strong positive effect, conforming with the need this demonimation has historically felt to have its own schools. That state per capita income D_2 has a positive effect on enrollment and school participation in the Title I poverty-related program D_3 has a negative effect both suggest that private education is a normal economic good whose consumption varies directly with income. In none of the part A regressions was the dummy variable for the year statistically significant, thus it was not included in the final regressions; this finding suggests that no exogenous decline in demand for private elementary schooling occurred during the 1976–1978 period.

The tuition coefficients are of primary importance. As theory implies, all the tuition coefficients are negative and significant. Of greater importance is the fact that the TSLS estimate of the tuition coefficient is considerably more negative than the OLS estimate in identical regressions (compare 2.1.1 with 2.1.2). This suggests that tuition and enrollment are jointly determined, thereby providing support for models E and EQ but not R.

Regression 2.1.3 is similar to 2.1.2 except that an interaction variable I has been included to test the hypothesis that demand elasticities with respect to tuition may vary between poverty-area markets and other markets. If, as sometimes alleged, public schools in poverty neighborhoods are inferior to those in other areas, we might expect public schools to be a poorer substitute for private schools in poverty areas than elsewhere; thus the demand elasticity should be smaller in poverty neighborhoods. Having found that the interaction

---

one standard deviation below mean for low-income market. For regressions with interaction term, $dE/dT = B_1 + B_2 D_i$, where B_1 = coefficient of tuition; B_2 = coefficient of interaction term, and D_i = nontuition variable D_2 or D_3. Obtaining tuition elasticity in equations that include interaction terms requires evaluating this derivative (conventionally at means) and multiplying by ratio of mean tuition to mean enrollment.

b. Definition of T is broader than in other regressions because other revenues (per pupil) of private schools are added to T.

variable has a significant coefficient, one may utilize
the respecified equation to calculate demand elasticities
with respect to tuition for different values of Title I
participation, where Title I participation is the proxy
for poverty. As the calculated elasticities for 2.1.3
show, the demand elasticity is much smaller when the
Title I variable is set one standard deviation above its
mean value. This result is consistent with the hypothesis that potential users of private schools in poverty
areas are less sensitive to changes in tuition than
others.

The first three regressions in part A use the nominal definition of tuition. Regressions 2.1.4 and 2.1.5
use the broader definition. By usual criteria, the broad
definition of tuition can be said to explain enrollment
demand better than the nominal definition. The R^2
statistic is larger in these latter two regressions.
Further, the t-statistics for the coefficients of the
broad definition of tuition are somewhat larger than for
the nominal definition. A possible implication of this
is that private elementary schools may receive payments
in lieu of larger nominal tuition payments. This finding
makes economic sense for there is no tax advantage under
current law to making tuition payments, although there is
an advantage in making payments in lieu of tuition as tax-
deductible donations to private schools or to their
sponsoring organizations. That the statistical result
is consistent with this hypothesis does not prove the
hypothesis, of course.

The results of part B tell a similar story. Coefficients have the expected signs and are highly significant; they are even of approximately the same magnitude
as those in part A. The only exception to this is that
the tuition coefficients (nominal tuition) are much
larger in B than in A because of the difference in mean
tuition levels between the two samples (see appendix to
this chapter); the elasticities, which effectively net
out differences in coefficient magnitudes caused by differences in tuition size, are of approximately the same
magnitude for comparable regressions in parts A and B.

The qualitative similarities between A and B extend
to other issues. In part B, as in A, comparison of TSLS
with OLS estimates of the tuition coefficient suggest
simultaneity bias, implying that models E or EQ are the
best representations of the market for private elementary
education. In addition, the effect of an interaction

variable in 2.1.8 in part B is similar to the effect of the interaction variable in regressions in part A. Specifically, the interaction term is statistically significant, and the enrollment demand elasticity with respect to tuition is less sensitive to tuition changes (less negative) in poorer market areas. (The sign of the interaction variable in part A is positive but in B is negative because tuition in A was multiplied by a poverty variable, Title I, and tuition in B was multiplied by an income variable; the Title I variable was not available for the part B regressions.) Both studies of elementary schooling, then, tend to support the view that substitution for private education is less feasible in poorer market areas than elsewhere.

Part C presents the demand functions for all secondary private schooling in the period 1976–1978. Regressions 2.1.9 and 2.1.10 are identical except that one is estimated by OLS and the other by TSLS. In contrast to parts A and B, these regressions show no evidence of simultaneity, the coefficients being very similar in size. If the supply functions for this sample also fail to find evidence of the joint determination of tuition and enrollment, the appropriateness of models E or EQ would be put in question; since the rationing model R would be the logical alternative, one would have to question even the possibility of estimating a demand function. Although it would be premature to conclude that model R should be chosen as the preferred model for secondary private education until the rest of the evidence is reviewed, note that variables D_1, D_2, and D_3 are omitted from regressions 2.1.9 and 2.1.10 because of their failure to behave according to theoretical expectations in the underlying reduced-form wage equation. (Regressions 2.1.9 and 2.1.10 are identified by the regional dummy variables found to play a role as demand variables in the underlying reduced-form wage and enrollment regressions.) While this might tend to support model R, which implies that a demand regression cannot be estimated, we find, nevertheless, that the magnitude of the demand elasticity is similar to those found in parts A and B.

An alternative definition of tuition might provide more support for models E or EQ. Regressions 2.1.11 and 2.1.12 present results for the broad definition of tuition. Of significance is that in regression 2.1.11 the state income variable D_2 resumes its role as a demand

variable (as ascertained by its behavior in the underlying reduced-form regressions). The continued failure
of D_1 (Catholic population) and D_3 (Title I) to perform
as demand variables is of less concern, for the desire
to provide religious values through education may be more
diluted by other motives at the secondary than at the
primary level, and the participation of secondary schools
in Title I is so much less than that of elementary
schools that Title I is a doubtful proxy for location of
the school in a poverty area.

The tuition elasticity in regression 2.1.11 is
highly significant and is of approximately the same magnitude as reported for the elementary schools. Regression
2.1.12 includes an interaction variable (the broad measure of tuition multiplied by D_2, state income); the interaction variable, however, is not significant and adds
nothing to the R^2 of the regression. Further, the tuition elasticity of enrollment demand calculated with income set one standard deviation below its mean value is
virtually identical to the elasticity calculated with all
variables at their means. The implication is that in the
secondary market the tuition elasticity of enrollment demand is the same across submarkets (defined by income).
This is the opposite of our finding for elementary markets.
An explanation for this resides in the underlying theoretical justification for tuition elasticities differing
across income groups. The original hypothesis was that
in low-income areas public schools might be viewed as
poor substitutes for private schools, making lower (less
negative) demand elasticities with respect to tuition in
poorer neighborhoods. That the hypothesis is not borne
out for secondary schools suggests that public high
schools are reasonably good substitutes for private high
schools.

This difference in findings between elementary and
secondary schooling makes some sense when we consider the
way in which curriculum is divided at the elementary and
secondary levels. Elementary students are generally required to cover a curriculum that is not highly differentiated, but at the secondary level there are major
divisions into vocational, general, and academic "tracks."
Thus, private elementary schools in higher income communities may compete directly with rather good public
schools; but private elementary schools in poorer communities compete with poorer public schools. However, at
the high school level, private schools typically compete

only with the academic track in the public high schools.
If admission to the public school academic curriculum is
selective, the ability of students and the kinds of de-
mands made upon them in the academic track may well
approximate that found in many private secondary schools.
This would tend to make the academic track at public
schools a fairly good substitute for private schools,
even in low-income markets.

The results for Roman Catholic secondary schools in
the period 1968-1970 are given in part D. The problems
associated with part C have disappeared. Specifically,
the conventional demand variables D_1 and D_2 (data for D_3
are not available for this sample) are again statistically significant, with expected signs; in addition, the
tuition variable has a significant and negative coefficient. Comparison of OLS and TSLS (2.1.13 and 2.1.14)
again reveal the existence of simultaneous equations
bias; that is, the OLS coefficient is much closer to zero
than the TSLS coefficient. These findings tend to support the view that the market for secondary private education may not be very different from the market for
elementary private education.

Part D produces one result that is clearly at vari-
ance with results for all of the other three studies. The
demand elasticity with respect to tuition in the preferred TSLS 2.1.14 is a very large -2.1. Nowhere else
have we found such a large (negative) demand elasticity.
The reason is not entirely clear, but a larger elasticity
at the secondary than at the elementary level might be
expected if the parents' motive to inculcate religious
beliefs is stronger at the elementary level than at the
secondary. Public schools, which maintain neutrality on
religious matters, may thus be considered a poor substitute for parochial schools at the elementary level; but
at the secondary level other parental motives may domi-
nate (e.g., How good are chances for college admission?
How good are laboratories?) making the public schools
better substitutes. A larger demand elasticity could be
expected, therefore, at the secondary level.

Finally, 2.1.15 contains an interaction term (tuition multiplied by state per capita income). The coefficient of the interaction term is not significant; it
is so small that the elasticity calculated for a low-
income market is virtually the same as for the mean market. This result is compatible with that in part C; at
the secondary level there is no evidence of difference

in enrollment demand elasticity with respect to tuition
across different markets specified by income level. This
finding clearly differentiates between demand patterns
of elementary and secondary levels.

Recap of Demand Results
        The four demand studies have produced results that
are significant and largely consistent. It would appear
that the evidence supports the following hypotheses for
private elementary education:

        1. The enrollment demand for private schooling has
an elasticity with respect to tuition of about -0.4.
        2. Tuition and enrollment are simultaneously
determined, i.e., a model like E or EQ is the appropriate
representation of the market.
        3. The demand elasticity is smaller (less sensi-
tive to tuition changes) in low-income markets than elsewhere.
        4. A broader definition of tuition performs at
least as well as the nominal definition in explaining
enrollment demand.

Hypothesis 1 is of significance, for a demand elasticity
less than zero means that a tuition tax credit that has
the effect of lowering the net tuition payment of parents
must increase the enrollment for private education.
Hypothesis 2 is of significance, for it is inconsistent
with the claim that the market for private education is
characterized by nonprice rationing, making economic
analysis of the market, if not impossible, markedly more
difficult than of conventional markets.[9] Hypothesis 3
will be of importance in evaluating the claim that a
tuition tax credit may change the socioenomic enrollment
patterns in private schools. Finally, hypothesis 4 implies that hidden tuition charges may exist for elementary schooling. If they do, the enactment of a tuition
tax credit would provide the incentive for schools and
parents to convert such hidden charges into explicit
charges, with obvious results for the cost to the government of a tuition tax credit.
        For secondary private education the following
findings may be stated:

        1. An enrollment elasticity with respect to

tuition has been found, although its magnitude may be as large as -2.1 or as small as -0.4.

2. In one secondary market the evidence of simulaneity favors model E or EQ while in the other it does not (final judgment awaits the evidence of the supply regressions).

3. The demand elasticity appears to be the same across markets differentiated by income.

4. The broader definition of tuition performs better than the nominal definition in explaining secondary enrollment demand.

SUPPLY FUNCTIONS

The regression estimates of the supply functions for three of the four private-education markets under discussion are presented in Table 2.2. No results are reported for the Roman Catholic elementary schools, 1968-1970, because no plausible estimates of a supply rela-

Table 2.2. Supply of Nonpublic Education (dependent variable: enrollment as proportion of age group)

Con-stant	S_1	S_2	S_3	S_4	T	R	Y	No.	R^2	Type	Regr.
A. Nonpublic elementary, 1976-78											
- 3.7	-.01	.008	.04	.00004	-.002			98	.754	OLS	2.2.1
	(0.3)	(1.7)	(1.6)	(0.7)	(1.4)						
- 8.7	.06	.01**	.03	.00008	.004			98	.754	TSLS	2.2.2
	(1.3)	(2.5)	(1.2)	(1.2)	(1.5)						
					[0.24]						
- 5.6	.07	...	.02	.00009	.004a			98	.742	TSLS	2.2.3
	(1.7)		(0.8)	(1.5)	(1.4)						
					[0.37]						
B. Nonpublic secondary, 1976-78											
- 7.6	.154*	...	.020	-.000004	.004*			100	.536	OLS	2.2.4
	(3.4)		(1.8)	(0.3)	(4.6)						
					[0.67]						
-19.1	.384*		.019*	.000004	.011*			100	.783	TSLS	2.2.5
	(10.2)		(2.6)	(0.4)	(12.3)						
					[1.95]						
-27.1	.4*		.05*	-.00005*	.01*a			100	.825	TSLS	2.2.6
	(11.2)		(6.5)	(4.2)	(13.3)						
					[2.3]						
C. Catholic secondary, 1968-70											
-10.4	.1*		.02**	-.000006	.003			84	.667	OLS	2.2.7
	(5.4)		(2.4)	(0.5)	(1.0)						
					[0.1]						
-23	.2*		.02*	-.00001	.049*		-1.1*	84	.827	TSLS	2.2.8
	(10.5)		(3.8)	(1.6)	(8.3)		(3.0)				
					[1.7]						

Coefficients times 10^{-2} = regression coefficients; t-values ( ); elasticities [ ].
Definitions of variables: S_1 = % of private teachers from religious orders; S_2 = nontuition revenues per pupil; S_3 = ave. enrollment; S_4 = ave. enrollment^2; T = ave. nominal tuition, except where indicated; R = region dummy variables, coefficients omitted; Y = year dummy variable, included in regression only if significant.
Levels of significance: *significant at greater than 1%, two-side test; **significant at greater than 5%, two-side test.
aBroad definition of tuition.

tionship (i.e., no positive relation between tuition and enrollment supply) were found. The exogenous variables S_1 through S_4 represent, respectively, a proxy for lowered input costs (percent of teachers in religious orders), a proxy for subsidization of costs (nontuition revenue per pupil), and two proxies for scale factors (average enrollment and the square of average enrollment). Several regional dummy variables were found in the underlying reduced-form regressions to be primarily supply-side variables (or neutral without a clear demand or supply orientation); however, for economy of space and because these coefficients are not subject to much interpretation, they are not reported. The supply-side regional dummy variables presumably capture such effects as regional differences in the regulations under which private schools operate (thereby imposing costs) or differences in input costs (such as teachers' salaries). Both nominal tuition and the broad tuition variables are used and results reported.

Table 2.2 is more easily discussed than Table 2.1, for fewer special hypotheses are being tested on the supply side; it is even possible to discuss the three parts together. First, in all three parts, the TSLS estimate of the tuition coefficient is more positive than the OLS estimate, which in one case is even negative. This evidence supports the view that tuition and enrollment are jointly determined by a market-clearing process as modeled by E or EQ. It is particularly significant that the evidence of simultaneity appears in the supply functions estimated for secondary schools in the 1976-1978 period (part B), as the demand regressions for this sample were the only ones that failed to support the hypothesis that tuition and enrollment were jointly determined. Given this result in the supply regressions, there appears to be little reason to support model R, the rationing model of the market for private schooling.

Second, the supply elasticities reported in Table 2.2 are remarkably consistent within sectors. The preferred TSLS estimates of the supply elasticity with respect to tuition in both secondary markets are approximately +2. Third, the supply elasticity in the reported elementary market is highly inelastic for either the nominal or broad definition of tuition. Further, the tuition coefficients in part A are only marginally significant at the 10 percent level on a one-side test. This inelasticity is consistent with the unreported results

for the parochial elementary market in which no positive
coefficients were found. It is difficult to conclude
with confidence that the elementary supply elasticity is
not zero, even though the best estimate is about +0.2.

Why this extreme supply inelasticity? The answer
may lie in our samples' exceptionally low average elementary tuition charges, which are insufficient to cover
costs. (See Table 1.4; also, compare expenditures,
Table 1.3, with tuition revenue, Table 2.A.1.) The regression equations capture the supply response to tuition
variations in a range that is too low to cover costs;
tuition charges that are below per pupil costs hardly
provide an incentive to expand pupil places. Obviously,
existing schools rely on subsidies; in addition to explicit subsidies (Table 1.4) implicit subsidies are present in the form of existing capital that imposes no
drain on the·current budget, but that could not be obtained except at high cost by any new school. If potential new private elementary schools are unlikely to have
access to the subsidies enjoyed by established schools,
they would have to rely almost entirely on tuition revenue to cover costs. The tuition levels actually observed
in our samples would permit few new schools to cover
costs. Thus, the supply function is highly inelastic.
It is likely that at much higher tuition levels a greater
supply elasticity might be observed. However, there is
no reason to doubt that our regressions accurately reflect the supply response of the current elementary
market.

The independent supply variables, though sometimes
not highly significant, have the expected signs. Variables
S_1 and S_2, which lower the cost curves, imply increased
supply of enrollment, all else equal. The scale terms S_3
and S_4 together show a positive impact of scale on the
enrollment in the current average range of enrollments;
this would be expected if larger scale were inversely related to cost for the size schools with which we are
dealing.

Of some interest is the single case where the dummy
variable for the year proved to be significant (2.2.8).
The negative and significant coefficient of the year variable for Catholic secondary schools in the late 1960s
suggests that some factor other than thoese explicitly
controlled was reducing the supply of places in Catholic
high schools. This suggestion is consistent with the
declining enrollment trends in Catholic schools at the

time and with the assertions by school administrators of
that time that the trend was not a demand-side phenomenon.
It is likely some factor related to costs or decreased
subsidization beyond the factors we have succeeded in
controlling.

The supply functions in Table 2.2 permit the
following conclusions:

1. The supply functions support the view that tuition and enrollment are jointly determined, thereby sup-
porting models E or EQ.

2. A positive supply elasticity with respect to
tuition in the secondary sector of about 2.0 has been
found.

3. The supply elasticity for the elementary sector
is very inelastic, possibly zero, with a best estimate of
about +0.2.

CONCLUSION

Research on the market for private education has
been long neglected, perhaps because of a belief that the
data requirements for estimating demand and supply equations in a nonclearing market were too difficult to be
met.   This study has shown that for the two periods
studied the private markets seem to behave as though they
cleared, with tuition and enrollment jointly determined.
Both demand and supply elasticities have been obtained,
which will make possible an informed analysis of the impact of a tuition tax credit on the private-education
market.

APPENDIX TO CHAPTER 2

DATA SOURCES AND DEFINITIONS

The major source of data for the 1976-1978 period
was the National Center for Education Statistics
(NCES) data tape from the Nonpublic Elementary and Secondary School Survey for Three Years (1976-1979).   Data
are reported for individual private schools (13,029
elementary and 2517 secondary) on items such as tuition
revenue, other revenue, enrollment, participation in the

federal Title I program, and faculty composition. Because the unit of observation in this study is the state market, not the individual school, individual school data were aggregated over states using the Statistical Package for the Social Sciences (SPSS) adapted to a Hewlett-Packard 3000 computer.

The dependent variable is private enrollment in each state, which is obtained by aggregating school enrollment data, and dividing by population in the relevant age group (5- to 13-year olds for the elementary study and 14- to 17-year olds for the secondary study). State populations by age groups were obtained from various issues of *Statistical Abstracts of the United States.*

The important tuition variable for the 1976-1978 studies was obtained by aggregating tuition revenues by state and dividing by aggregated enrollments; this average tuition was figured with data from schools reporting nonzero values for both tuition revenues and enrollment on the NCES tape. Relatively few schools were missing data for both tuition and enrollment, in part due to the imputation of values by NCES in many cases where schools failed to reply to sections of the questionnaire. By dealing with tuition revenues divided by enrollment, various problems associated with tuition rates were avoided (e.g., how to deal with scholarships that reduce actual tuition below stated rates).

Other variables obtained by aggregation from the data tape were the proportion of teachers in religious orders (religious teachers divided by total faculty), other revenue per pupil (aggregated other revenue divided by enrollment), average school enrollment, and proportion of schools reporting participation in Title I.

Two demand variables were obtained from generally published sources: State per capita income was obtained from various issues of *Statistical Abstracts of the United States*. Roman Catholic population figures by state were obtained from the *Catholic Almanac,* 1976 and 1981 editions, and from the 1961 *Official Catholic Directory* (interpolation was used between years); this figure was then stated as a proportion of state populations.

In all cases of variables denoted in money terms, the second-year data in the pair of pooled years in the sample was deflated to the first-year price level.

Pooling pairs of years to obtain larger samples suggested using a dummy variable for time. The year

dummy appeared in underlying reduced-form regressions
but was omitted when insignificant in structural regressions.

Two sets of regional dummy variables were used:
Central, South and West for the elementary (1976-1978)
study, and a larger set of New England, Mid-Atlantic,
Midwest, Plains, Southwest, and Northwest for the Catholic
elementary and secondary studies. The larger set was
suggested by the way data on Catholic schools is grouped
in National Catholic Education Association publications.
The smaller set preserved degrees of freedom in preliminary runs, with smaller samples for individual years, and
performed as well as the larger set in the pooled sample
for elementary schools 1976-1978.

For the two studies on Roman Catholic schools in
the 1968-1970 period, state enrollment figures, already
aggregated were obtained from the National Catholic Educational Association (NCEA) *Statistical Report on
Catholic Elementary and Secondary Schools for the Years
1967-1968 to 1969-1970* (Washington, D.C.: 1970). This
report also provided data on faculty composition and permitted calculation of average school size. The NCEA does
not publish tuition data by state; this was obtained from
the appendix of the report prepared for the President's
Commission on School Finance by Notre Dame University.
Other variables, such as percent of population that is
Catholic, were as reported above.

All variables used in the 1968-1970 study were
made as comparable as possible to the 1976-1978 study.
Note that no variable comparable to Title I was found
for the earlier period. Since neither the NCES nor the
Notre Dame group exhaustively document what one labels
"current tuition and fees" and the other labels simply
"tuition and fees," some differences in definition may
persist.

The sample sizes for the four studies vary, although
the secondary-school sample for 1976-1978 numbers all
fifty states for two years. The elementary study for
1976-1978 did not include the state of Missouri when it
was found without apparent cause that the average enrollment was significantly smaller in the second of the two
years, suggesting some kind of error in the data. The
samples for Catholic schools are substantially smaller,
primarily because tuition revenues were not reported for
all states. In addition, due to the overlapping of
diocesan boundaries and state lines, Maryland, Delaware,

Table 2.A.1. Sample Mean Values of Major Regression Variables

Variable	1976-78 Elementary	1976-78 Secondary	1968-70 Catholic Elementary	1968-70 Catholic Secondary
Enrollment (proportion)	0.073	0.056	0.084	0.056
Tuition	392	994	41	193
Per pupil other revenue	241.6	372	...	...
Per capita income (00)	62.9	62.8	32.5	32.4
Title I participation (%)	39.1	18.0	...	...
Religious teachers (%)	21.1	21.0	52.3	54.1
Average enrollment per school	196	351	305	387

and Washington, D.C. were aggregated in the studies of Catholic schools.

Mean values of all important variables are given in Table 2.A.1. These mean values are state weighted, not school or enrollment weighted. State weighted means are not necessarily the correct means to use if one is interested in national means.

NOTES

1. Demand elasticities of very small magnitude for individual schools, not markets, were reported by Daniel Sullivan, *Public Aid to Nonpublic Schools* (Lexington, Mass.: Heath, 1974). *Economic Problems of Nonpublic Schools: Report to the President's Commission on School Finance*; ed. Frank J. Fahey (Notre Dame, Ind.: Notre Dame Univ., 1972), reported no successes in several attempts to find demand elasticities for private schools. As recently as 1981, James Coleman et al., *Public and Private Schools*, first draft (Chicago, Ill.: Nat. Opinion Res. Center, 1981), 75, claimed no knowledge of the responsiveness of enrollment demand to tuition changes. Recently, O. Homer Erekson, "Equity Targets in School Finance, Tuition Tax Credits, and The Public-Private Choice," *Journal of Education Finance*, 7(4), 446, reported--contrary to economic theory--a positive enrollment demand elasticity for parochial schools, and a very small negative demand elasticity for nonparochial, private schools. Correspondence with several associations of private schools failed to discover any demand and supply studies.

2. In a quasi-equilibrium market, the true demand equation (2.2) could be estimated only if data on appli-

cations rather than enrollment were available; no compre-
hensive source on applications is available.

    3. This assumes that the covariance between the
random terms in the demand and supply equations is zero.
See G. S. Maddala, *Econometrics* (New York: McGraw-Hill,
1977), 242-249.

    4. Richard B. Freeman, in *Labor in the Public and
Nonprofit Sectors*, ed. D. Hamermesh (Princeton, N. J.:
Princeton Univ. Press, 1975), 88-89.

    5. On scale economies in education, see Elchanan
Cohn, *The Economics of Education*, rev. ed. (Cambridge,
Mass.: Ballinger, 1979), 202.

    6. Sullivan, 22, 43-44.

    7. Whether donations in lieu of tuition are proper-
ly tax deductible may depend on the specific details of
tuition and donations. If a parent personally received
a dollar-for-dollar tuition reduction in return for a
donation, the Internal Revenue Service (IRS) would dis-
allow the deduction. However, if all donations were
pooled to provide uniformly low tuition for all (even
those who did not contribute), the donations might be
deductible; the less directly any benefits are related
to donations and the more voluntary the donations, the
stronger the case for deductibility. The issue here,
however, is not what forms of donations in lieu of higher
tuition charges should be allowed as deductions. The
economic hypothesis is that possible deductibility provides the incentive to convert tuition into donations
and that parents would adjust enrollment demand to a perceived cost of both tuition and such "donations." The
statistical analyses of this chapter do not depend on the
exact details of the hypothesized conversion of tuition
into donations nor on any judgments about what ought to
be allowed as a deduction.

    8. *Economic Problems of Nonpublic Schools: Report
to the President's Commission on School Finance*, ed. F. J.
Fahey (Notre Dame, Ind.: Notre Dame Univ., 1972).

    9. See William T. Garner and Jane Hannaway, in
Family Choice in Schooling, ed. M. Manley-Casimir
(Lexington, Mass.: Heath, 1982), 121.

CHAPTER 3

Cost and Distribution of Benefits

CONCEPTUAL FRAMEWORK

The most important policy question asked about tuition tax credits is how much they will cost when fully implemented. Because a credit would take effect in a future year, any estimate of its cost in lost tax revenues to the federal government would be problematical. A next-best approach asks how much the credit would have cost if it had been in effect during some recent year for which necessary data on the private education sector exist. The analyst would find the average per pupil credit as some percent c (up to a maximum) of tuition prevailing during that year multiplied by private-school enrollments for that year to obtain the estimated revenue loss to the government. Additional adjustments would be made if the credit were not refundable or if the credit were to be phased out for families with incomes above some level. However, the basic method is straightforward.

Unfortunately, this method is almost certain to produce an underestimate of the actual cost of a tuition tax credit. Economic theory suggests that a tuition subsidy, such as the tax credit, would stimulate increases of both tuition and enrollment in the private sector; that is, tuition and enrollment figures actually observed in a year for which no subsidy was in effect would be smaller than they would be with a credit. The only case in which a tuition subsidy would not induce increases in tuition and enrollment would be if the demand elasticity for private schooling was zero. (This extreme assumption is not supported by the evidence presented in chapter 2.)

The general case of a tuition tax credit is illustrated in Fig. 3.1. Since the credit is a subsidy to de-

manders, the impact of a credit of 50 percent may be
viewed as shifting the demand curve vertically so that the
original demand curve D lies halfway between the horizontal
axis and the new demand curve D'. If the maximum credit
is $500, the curve D' will be parallel to D for all tui-
tion levels greater than $1000. (If the credit were, say,
25 percent, the curve D' would be displaced so that D
would lie three-fourths of the distance between the axis
and D', etc.) The effect of a credit imposed on a system
is to move the market-clearing equilibrium from point A to
B. This implies an increase in tuition from T_0 to T_1 and
of enrollment from E_0 to E_1. If T_1 exceeded T_0 by the
full amount of the credit, the task of finding the new
equilibrium would be trivial. However, in general the
tuition level will not increase by the full amount of the
credit. Parents pay neither T_0 nor T_1 but $T_1 - C$. Fig.
3.1 also reveals that an inelastic supply function (tending to the vertical) would convert the demand stimulus of
the credit largely into tuition effects, while an elastic
supply function (tending to the horizontal) would produce
primarily enrollment increases. In general though, a
credit would produce both higher enrollment and tuition
levels. Therefore, estimates of the cost of a credit that
fail to account for the credit's enhancement of tuition
and enrollment will be underestimates.

    Fig. 3.1 shows that the only condition under which

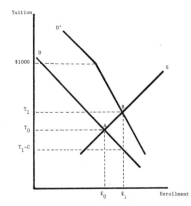

Fig. 3.1. Displacement of market equilibrium due to
tuition tax credit. (For tuition greater than $1000,
D' will be parallel to D with vertical distance of $500
between because of $500 cap.)

a tuition tax credit would fail to induce increases in tuition, enrollment, or both is the condition of a vertical demand curve (i.e., zero demand elasticity); in that case D' is superimposed on D so that both curves intersect the supply curve at the same equilibrium point. Such cost estimates produce the lowest bound of feasible estimates.

This chapter presents elasticity-based estimates of the cost of several credit plans, using the elasticity estimates for demand and supply functions discussed in chapter 2. The formulas for new equilibrium tuition levels T_1 are derived in the appendix to this chapter. The elasticity-based cost figures are contrasted with a set of zero elasticity (lowest-bound) cost estimates published in a recent benchmark study.

The zero demand elasticity assumption produces cost estimates by assuming the per pupil credit to be c percent of T_0 (actual tuition prevailing in the benchmark year) multiplied by E_0 (actual number of students enrolled that year). The elasticity-based estimates require values for T_1 and E_1; the cost estimate is then c percent of T_1 multiplied by E_1 (cT_1E_1). Since T_1 is never directly observed, one must rely on what might be called the fundamental relationship between T_0 and T_1 discussed in detail in the appendix:

$$T_1 = T_0/(1 - cM)$$

The term M is the absolute value of the demand elasticity divided by the sum of the absolute values of the elasticities of demand and supply.

COMPARISON WITH 1978 BENCHMARK STUDY

In much of what follows our discussion refers to a benchmark study that utilized the zero demand elasticity methods to calculate the cost of a hypothetical 1978 tuition tax credit of 50 percent (up to $500 maximum).[1] This study utilized survey data from the October 1978 Current Population Survey to find the median tuition T_0 actually paid by private students that year and the actual levels of enrollment E_0. The tuition levels were multiplied by 50 percent to find the hypothetical average credit up to $500 received per pupil; this was multiplied by the number of students to obtain the total cost. The

Table 3.1. Cost Estimates for Hypothetical Credit for 50%, $500 Maximum: 1978

	Enrollment (000)	Median Tuition ($)	Median Credit ($)	Cost ($000)	Excess over Low-bound Cost (%)
A. Zero elasticity, low-bound estimates[a]					
Elementary	3233	356	178	575,474	...
Secondary	1244	901	451	561,044	...
Total				1,136,518	
B. Elasticity-based estimates for nominal tuition[b]					
Elementary	3556	534	267	949,452	65
Secondary	1470	983	491	721,770	29
Total				1,671,222	47
C. Elasticity-based estimates for broad definition of tuition[c]					
Elementary	3781	812	406	1,535,086	166
				(1,286,145)[d]	(123)
Secondary	1371	1291	500	685,500	22
				(539,952)	(-4)
Total				2,220,586	95

[a]Benchmark, zero elasticity study reported in Martha J. Jacobs, Table 1 (see Note 1). Tuition and enrollment figures are actual. Median tuition figures are similar to 1977-78 values in appendix in chapter 2.
[b]For elementary schools, demand elasticity = -0.4; supply elasticity = +0.2. For secondary, demand elasticity = -0.4; supply elasticity = +2.0.
[c]For elementary schools, demand elasticity = -1.0; supply = 0.4. For secondary, demand elasticity = -0.4; supply = 2.3.
[d]Figures in parentheses assume government recoups tax deductible donations in lieu of tuition before tax credit. Average top tax bracket for deductions is 35%.

credit was assumed refundable so that no adjustment was needed for families with insufficient tax liability to benefit. The level of tuition was based on the replies of the respondents, who presumably quoted only nominal tuition.

Table 3.1 provides three distinct estimates of the cost of the hypothetical credit. Part A shows the major findings of the benchmark study. The median credit is one-half of actual median tuitions T_0 charged that year, and total cost is actual enrollment E_0 multiplied by this. This produces a cost estimate of $1.14 billion. In A the full credit is retained by the parents; i.e., under zero elasticity assumptions the equilibrium level of tuition does not rise and the schools cannot capture any of the credit from the parents.

Part B presents an estimate of tuition T_1, enrollment E_1, size of credit, and total costs based on values of demand and supply elasticities developed in chapter 2. In B, as in A, the nominal definition of tuition is used; the most conservative elasticity estimates are used. The statistic that best summarizes the differences between A and B is the total cost figure, which at $1.68 billion is fully 47 percent larger in B. This result is due to increases of both tuition and enrollment levels: a larger average credit would be received by more students.

Recalling that part A tuition figures are actual T_0 figures for 1978, we see that B implies elementary tuition is boosted to a T_1 value, \$534, that is about 50 percent larger than T_0; and secondary tuition is boosted by about 9 percent. Secondary tuition is boosted much less in proportionate terms because the supply elasticity for secondary private education is much larger than for elementary private education and it channels most of the impact of the credit into larger enrollments rather than into higher tuition. Another way of stating the same thing is that elementary *schools* and secondary *parents* capture a good portion of the credit.[2]

Cost estimates based on the broad concept of tuition are reported in part C. The broad definition adds to average nominal tuition the average of other revenues collected per pupil. Some portion of these other revenues (e.g., endowment income, alumni donations) are conceptually unlike tuition; however, some portion of these other revenues may be paid by parents and be viewed by them as tuition payments, thus converting a portion of what would otherwise be non tax-deductible into a tax-deductible "donation" to the school (or to an affiliated organization that channels the payment to the school).[3] Part C is calculated on the assumption that the value of a tax credit (50 percent of tuition) would be greater than the value of a tax deduction--the deduction's value depends on a taxpayer's bracket, which generally is much lower than 50 percent. If the credit is worth more than the deduction, deductible donations would be dropped and the schools would charge a level of tuition equal to the broad definition.

Note that C is calculated on the assumption that all "other revenue" belongs in the category of parental donations. Since some of this revenue comes from sources like endowments, C is an upper estimate of this practice's effects. Conversely, B, which uses the narrow definition of tuition, assumes that none of schools' other revenue should be treated as though it were in effect tuition and is the lower estimate.

To calculate C, it was necessary to estimate the per pupil values of other revenue. These were assumed to be the same proportion of nominal tuition reported in the appendix to chapter 2, that is, 62 percent of nominal tuition for elementary schools and 37 percent for secondary schools.

The calculations of C are done in two steps. First, it is assumed that in order to obtain the credit all deductible donations must be given up; thus a hypothetical value of T_0 is constructed to show what tuition would have been if parents had not taken a tax subsidy through the deduction method. Second, we find the impact of the 50 percent credit as applied to this hypothetical value of T_0 (see the appendix to this chapter).

This two-step process reflects the cost of the credit to the government. A portion of the cost of the credit is offset by a discontinuation of tax deductible donations; therefore in C, the costs of the credit are given twice. Estimates outside parentheses show the cost of the credit without allowing for discontinued deductions; estimates inside parentheses allow for this offset. It is assumed that the deductions were claimed by families in an average tax bracket of 35 percent.

It is of great significance that the greater costs shown in C reflect the impact of the elementary sector entirely. (By one estimate the secondary sector costs are 4 percent less than in A.) The reason goes to the heart of the logic of the process: the $500 maximum on the size of the credit prevents the secondary credit from rising much beyond its value in B, or even A, whereas the elementary credit, which is still below the limit, rises dramatically. The result is that a $500 maximum credit provides secondary parents a smaller percentage cost reduction in C than in A or B. Because the credit is proportionately smaller in C than in B, its impact on enrollment is also smaller. Thus, while the per pupil secondary credit is actually slightly larger, far fewer students collect the credit--resulting in a smaller cost to the government.

This encounter is the first with what shall be seen as a pervasive effect of caps on credits: if a credit has reached its maximum, enrollment will begin to decline as tuition levels continue to rise and a capped credit becomes a smaller and smaller proportionate subsidy. It tends to reduce the government's revenue loss.

Part C also leads to the conclusion that if private schools and parents have two possible options--tax deductions and tax credits--a mixed strategy including both will maximize the amount of the subsidy once the credit has hit its maximum. When the tax credit is below its maximum, the credit is worth more than the deduction; thus, all donations intended to produce deductions would be incorporated into tuition. However, once the credit reaches its limit, it is in parents' interest to convert any tuition increases into donations again. For example, suppose the payment required by a school is $1200, to be paid either as tuition or a mixture of tuition and donations. If it is all taken as tuition, parents should receive a tax credit worth only the maximum $500. However, if the payment is taken as $1000 of tuition, plus a $200 donation, parents will receive a maximum $500 credit (50 percent of $1000) plus a tax deduction of $200, which has a value dependent on tax bracket.

In order to reduce complexity, C does not represent the results obtained from such a mixed strategy. Yet for the secondary sector, a mixed strategy would have been in order. Equilibrium tuition of $1291 in the secondary sector fully exploits the tax credit; therefore, additional gains could be made by converting some of the payments above $1000 into donations. The qualitative effect of this is by now clear: equilibrium payments to the schools (tuition plus donations) would be above even $1291; the parental net payment would drop below $791 ($1291 - $500); and enrollment would exceed 1,371,000. The cost to government of this mixed strategy would exceed any shown in Table 3.1.

Note again that the secondary tax credit is projected to cost 4 percent less in C than under zero elasticity assumptions of A when the figure in parentheses is used. This apparent anomaly is explained partly by the failure to calculate C on the basis of a mixed strategy. The tax deduction on donations is fully relinquished; at an assumed tax bracket of 35 percent this loses a tax deduction worth $116 per student. The net effect is that the total cost to the government may be less in C than in A. A mixed strategy would not have produced this result.

Table 3.1 allows several generalizations. One finds that elasticity-based estimates of the cost of a tuition tax credit run substantially higher than zero elasticity estimates, the supply elasticity plays a significant role in converting the stimulus of the credit into increased enrollment rather than tuition, and the broad definition of tuition produces cost increases that are potentially much larger than expected from an analysis based on zero elasticity assumptions coupled with the narrow definition of tuition. Finally, the table provides some evidence that the maximum on the credit may have the effect of

Table 3.2. Cost Estimates for Hypothetical Credit of 50%, $250 Maximum: 1978

	Enrollment (000)	Median Tuition ($)	Median Credit ($)	Cost ($000)	Excess over Low-bound Cost (%)
A. Zero elasticity low-bound estimates					
Elementary	3233	356	178	575,474	...
Secondary	1244	901	250	311,000	
Total				886,474	
B. Elasticity-based estimates for nominal tuition					
Elementary	3537	523	250	884,250	54
Secondary	1361	943	250	339,500	9.2
Total				1,223,750	38
C. Elasticity-based estimates for broad definition of tuition					
Elementary	3515	700	250	878,750 (629,809)[a]	53 (9.4)
Secondary	1282	1254	250	320,500 (174,952)[a]	3.1 (-44.3)
Total				1,199,250	35

[a]Assumes government recoups tax-deductible donations. Average top tax bracket for deductions is 35%.

substantially reducing the enrollment effects, and consequently the cost impacts, of a tuition tax credit.

Tax Credit with a Low Maximum

Table 3.2 reports alternative cost estimates for a tax credit of 50 percent with a maximum of only $250. Even in part A, the $250 limit has been reached for secondary education. Due to this limit, the cost to the government is smaller than if the maximum limit were higher or nonexistent. (Compare with Table 3.1, A.)

Whether one examines B (narrow tuition) or C (broad tuition), the results are similar. In each case, the total cost of the credit is approximately $1.2 billion, or about 38-39 percent larger than estimated under zero elasticity assumptions. This uniformity is due mainly to the low limit of $250, which keeps the per pupil credit the same in both B and C. The $250 credit represents a smaller proportion of tuition in C than in B, which tends to make the level of enrollment in C smaller; however, differences in elasticities generally offset this effect so that enrollments in B and C are similar.

Table 3.2 shows that even when limits on the size of the credit prevent its rising very far, zero elasticity estimates of the total revenue loss to the government still understate the true loss because they neglect enrollment effects. The exercise also suggests the importance of maximums on the credit to restrain the cost to the government. Comparison of Table 3.2 with Table 3.1 reveals this clearly. The savings are greater for B and C than for A because the $250 cap reduces both aver-

age credit size and enrollment in B and C but only the
size of the credit in A.

Progressive or Regressive?

The benchmark study of a hypothetical 1978 tax
credit also examined the distribution of benefits by income categories. A condensed version of those findings,
which concentrates on the share of benefits received by
families earning less than $10,000 in 1978 (Table 3.3,A)
shows that low-income families would receive 10.3 percent of all credit benefits paid by the government. By
comparison, low-income students constituted about 12 percent of private-school enrollment. Low-income secondary
students would receive about 8.7 percent of benefits,
while constituting about 10 percent of enrollment. Thus,
even under zero elasticity assumptions, low-income students receive a smaller share of benefits than their
share of the private school population because tuition
levels paid by low-income families are somewhat smaller
than the average for the total population.[4]

If demand and supply elasticities were the same
for all income categories of students, the shares of
benefits (but not dollar amounts) accruing to different
categories of students would be the same for all groups
(compare A and B). However, if low-income students have
a lower demand elasticity than the national average,
their share of credit benefits would be less than shown
in A. Since chapter 2 has shown that the demand elasticity for elementary (but not secondary) education is
actually smaller in low-income markets than elsewhere,
this is an important observation.

Table 3.3. Benefits to Low-Income Families from Hypothetical Credit of 50%, $500 Maximum: 1978

	Low-Income Enrollment in Private Schools		Low-Income Average	Low-Income Average	Benefits Paid to Low-Income Families	
	(000)	%	Tuition ($)	Credit ($)	($000)	% of total benefits
A. Zero elasticity estimates						
Elementary	388	12[a]	305[b]	153	59,364	10.3[c]
Secondary	124	10[a]	788[b]	394	48,856	8.7[c]
B. Elasticity-based estimates, for nominal definition of tuition						
Elementary[d]	414	11.6	406	203	84,042	8.9[c]
Secondary	147	10	860	430	63,210	8.7[c]

[a] Low income defined as less than $10,000 income and represents the three lowest income categories cited in Martha J. Jacobs, Table 4 (see note 1).

[b] Tuition is enrollment-weighted ave. 1978 tuition figures (Jacobs) for three lowest income categories.

[c] Ratio of col. 5 to total benefits given in Table 3.1, col. 4.

[d] The tuition elasticity of elementary enrollment demand is -0.2 for this row. All other elasticities in B are those of Table 3.1, B.

If all else is equal, a lower than average demand elasticity interacts with a tuition tax credit to produce two effects. Families with low demand elasticity will experience a proportionately smaller than average increase in tuition; therefore, they will obtain a smaller than average credit. Furthermore, the smaller credit will stimulate a smaller enrollment increase among low-income students. The consequence of these two effects is that a credit would (1) reduce the proportion of low-income students in private schools and (2) reduce their proportionate share of credit benefits even more.[5]

Part B is calculated on the assumption that the demand elasticity for elementary schooling is - 0.2, a figure consistent with the findings in chapter 2 (see Table 2.1) and about one-half as large as the average demand elasticity for elementary schooling used in Table 3.1,B. All other elasticities used in the calculation of B are the same as in Table 3.1; in particular, there was no evidence that secondary demand elasticities differed by income level. In B, as in A, shares of enrollment and of benefits are found by dividing the enrollment and benefit amounts for low-income students by the overall amounts.

The central finding of B is that at the elementary level low-income students would constitute 11.6 percent of private enrollment after enactment of a credit but would receive only about 8.9 percent of the benefits--even less than the 10.3 share under the zero elasticity assumptions of A. The finding makes sense, for a 50 percent credit will stimulate both tuition increases and enrollment increases for all categories of students, but the stimulation will be proportionately less for categories of students with smaller demand elasticities. Thus, while more low-income elementary students will be attending private schools after enactment of a credit, they would constitute a smaller portion of enrollment than before the credit; and their credit will also tend to be smaller than the average, resulting in a smaller share of benefits for them.

Part B also shows the effect expected for secondary students. Since demand elasticities are the same for all income groups, the credit had the effect of increasing both tuition and enrollment for all students equiproportionately, with no group gaining relative to others (compare A and B).

Part B shows that the major findings on distribution in the benchmark study, which used an oversimplified zero elasticity methodology, hold in an even stronger form. The benchmark study found that low-income students would obtain a less than proportionate share of credit benefits. Part B suggests that the proportion of benefits received by elementary students would be even smaller than suggested in A; the typical low-income elementary student would receive a credit benefit only 76.7 percent (8.9/11.6) that of the average private student. At the secondary level, the low-income student's benefit would be only 87 percent as large.[6]

Before leaving B, note that the benefits will be shared between the private-school families and the schools themselves. This is implicit in all calculations based on demand and supply elasticities: in general, schools will capture some of the credit benefits because the equilibrium level of tuition T_1 rises. This differs from A, where the zero elasticity assumption implies that all benefits accrue to the families.

No part C has been calculated for Table 3.3 because the degree to which low-income families might engage in the practice of making donations in lieu of tuition payments was not known; it seems likely that the tax advantages of such behavior would be small or nonexistent for low-income families.

PROJECTIONS FOR THE MID-1980s

Several proposals for tuition tax credits, including Reagan's 1982 and 1983 proposals, envision 1985 as the first year of full implementation. Suppose a 50 percent credit has a $500 limit and the credit is refundable, with no restrictions on eligibility because of family income. By making a few additional assumptions, it is possible to make projections of the 1985 costs of such a credit. Assume:

1. The elasticity estimates of chapter 2 continue to hold.
2. Tuition will remain constant in real dollars but double in nominal dollars between 1978 and 1985 (which corresponds to 10 percent annual inflation, compounded).
3. Enrollment in the absence of the credit (Table 3.4,A) can be extrapolated from current trends.[7]

Table 3.4. Cost of a 50% Refundable Tax Credit, $500 Maximum: 1985

	Projected Enrollment (000)	Projected Ave. Tuition ($)	Ave. Credit ($)	Total Cost ($000)	Deviation from Low-bound Estimates (%)
A. Zero elasticity, low-bound estimates					
Elementary	3453	712	356	1,229,268	
Secondary	1340	1802	500	670,000	
Total				1,899,268	
B. Elasticity-based estimates for nominal tuition					
Elementary	3777	1045	500	1,888,500	54
Secondary	1463	1885	500	731,500	9
Total				2,620,000	38
C. Elasticity-based estimates for nominal tuition with 25% state credits					
Elementary	3978	1254	500	1,989,000	62
Secondary	1586	1968	500	793,000	18
Total				2,782,000	46

Table 3.4,A, shows the enrollment, tuition, and cost
estimates for 1985 if a zero elasticity assumption holds.
The total cost to the government of the 1985 credit is
about $1.9 billion. This exceeds the comparable 1978
figure (Table 3.1,A) because both tuition and enrollment
are assumed to be somewhat larger.[8] Note that even though
tuition is assumed to be twice as large in 1985 as in
1978 and enrollment is somewhat larger, the cost to the
government has not doubled because the effect of the $500
maximum depresses the secondary credit far below what it
would have been otherwise.

The effect of considering demand and supply elasticities is apparent in B. The effect of the credit is
to increase both tuition and enrollment, with the total
cost to the government being 38 percent larger than projected in A. Close examination of B reveals that most
of the cost increase, from $1.9 billion to $2.6 billion,
is due to credit-induced enrollment increases, not tuition increases, because the $500 cap prevents the sec-
ondary credit from differing between A and B and prevents
the elementary credit from rising by more than $144 per
child.

The exercise of computing the cost to the government of a tuition tax credit assumes that the credit would
be constitutional. It is almost certain that if credit
were declared constitutional, numerous states would follow the federal government's lead. As a simple approxi-
mation, assume that by 1985 all states adopt 25 percent
tuition tax credits without maximum limits. If one ignores elasticity effects, state tuition tax credit should
have no impact on the cost of the federal program; however if elasticities are allowed for, state credits can
cause the cost of the federal programs to rise by about
$160 million (compare B and C). Although the federal

credit is at its maximum of $500 in both parts, enroll-
ment is larger in C than in B. Thus as state credits
decrease the net payments of parents (tuition minus both
credits), private-school enrollments increase. The result is an increase in the cost to the federal government
because of state actions; in C, the cost of the hypothetical 1985 credit is 46 percent larger than the estimated
costs of A.

The credit considered in Table 3.4 is similar to
credits proposed by both the administration and Senators
Packwood and Moynihan in 1982.

THE 1983 REAGAN PROPOSAL

In 1982 the Reagan administration proposed a credit
plan that did not pass Congress. A new plan was introduced in 1983. Because projected federal deficits were
exceptionally large, the administration proposed a very
modest credit of 50 percent with a low maximum of $300,
without refundability, and with a phaseout of benefits
for family incomes between $40,000 and $60,000. The
Congressional Research Service estimated this plan to
produce a revenue loss of $800 million per year when
fully implemented in 1985.

Table 3.5,A, was calculated on the basis of tuition
and enrollment projections consistent with Table 3.4

Table 3.5. Cost of a 50% Nonrefundable Credit, $300 Maximum and Phaseout: 1985

	Projected Enrollment (000)	Projected Ave. Tuition ($)	Ave. Credit ($)	Total Cost ($000)	Deviation from Low-bound Estimate (%)
A. Low-bound estimates					
Elementary (by income)					
$10,000-$40,000	1899	350	175	332,325	
$40,000-$60,000	1036	800	200	207,200	
Secondary (by income)					
$10,000-$40,000	617	650	300	184,800	
$40,000-$60,000	469	2000	200	93,800	
Total				818,125	
B. Elasticity-based estimates					
Elementary (by income)					
$10,000-$40,000	2089	525	262	547,318	
$40,000-$60,000	1070	933	200	214,000	
Secondary (by income)					
$10,000-$40,000	711	700	300	213,300	
$40,000-$60,000	484	2033	200	96,800	
Total				1,071,736	31
C. Elasticity-based with 25% state credits					
Elementary (by income)					
$10,000-$40,000	2237	657	300	671,100	
$40,000-$60,000	1119	1120	200	223,800	
Secondary (by income)					
$10,000-$40,000	769	730	300	230,700	
$40,000-$60,000	526	2122	200	105,200	
Total				1,230,800	50

except that enrollment is divided into income categories
relevant to the credit plan. Enrollment is allocated to
categories in which income is (1) less than $10,000, too
low to receive a nonrefundable credit; (2) between $10,000
and $40,000 per year, eligible for the maximum credit;
(3) $40,000 to $60,000, the range where the phaseout
occurs; and (4) above $60,000, too high to receive a
credit. The two categories ineligible for the credit
are omitted from the table. The proportions of total
enrollment assigned to each income category were obtained by adjusting actual 1979 proportions for expected inflationary effects on incomes.[9]

Average tuition figures, including those for income
brackets not reported, were projected such that (1) the
weighted average of tuition would equal the figure in
Table 3.4, (2) tuition and income would be positively
correlated, (3) the results should be plausible in light
of past experience. The average credit assigned to the
phaseout income range is $200 because any common income
distribution requires that most families in the range
would be nearer $40,000 than $60,000; thus, they would
receive a substantial portion of the maximum credit.

Part A follows a zero demand-elasticity methodology
and projects a revenue loss of $818 million per year--a
figure corresponding closely to the CRS estimate.

Part B shows the patterns of enrollment and tuition
that emerge from elasticity-based calculations. The
overall revenue loss is 31 percent larger than that in A
(and the government estimates). By now the reasons for
this are familiar to the reader.

Part C shows what happens if states follow the federal lead. Assuming 25 percent state credits with no
other restrictions, the revenue loss would be 50 percent
larger than projected in A. Note that this is the federal revenue loss alone. Any state revenue losses are
in addition to the losses given in C and are not dealt
with here. States influence the federal loss because
states are capable of stimulating enrollment by their
own credits; and all new students are eligible for the
federal credit.

Legislatures of states where private schools are
concentrated have in the past shown every inclination
to provide tax subsidies to private-school families--even
though the constitutionality of such subsidies is doubtful. If a federal tax credit is predicated on constitutionality, one must almost certainly assume the estab-

lishment of state credits. Part C, therefore, probably
gives a reasonable estimate of the annual cost of even
the relatively modest 1983 Reagan credit plan.

EFFECTS OF INFLATION ON CAPPED CREDITS
        Table 3.6 is designed to reveal the effects of in-
flation on a tax credit with a cap similar to the one in
Table 3.4. The table is based on the assumption that inflation will increase prices 140 percent between 1978 and
1985 instead of 100 percent as assumed in Table 3.4
(i.e., prices are 20 percent higher in Table 3.6 than in
Table 3.4). As in Table 3.4, tuition in Table 3.6,A, is
assumed to have just kept pace with general inflation so
that no real increase in tuition has occurred. Thus, the
projected enrollments in parts A of both tables are the
same; the inflationary increase in tuition has raised the
estimated credit costs from $1.9 billion to $2.1 billion
because of the larger credit for elementary students.
However, the secondary credit and enrollments do not
rise (the credit is $500 in both tables).[10]
        The most significant lesson comes from comparing
parts B in Tables 3.6 and 3.4. We find that inflation
has reduced the total cost to the government from $2.62
billion to $2.58 billion. This is only a $40 million
dollar decrease in nominal dollars; but recall that the
$2.58 billion of Table 3.6 is worth 20 percent less be-
cause of inflation, than the dollars in Table 3.4. This
demonstrates a rather surprising and strong result:
once a tax credit has hit its maximum, further inflationary increases in tuition reduce the cost to the federal
government in both nominal dollars and--even more--in
real dollars.
        If one comprehends the logic of the economic model,
this should not seem a paradox. Comparing parts B of
Tables 3.4 and 3.6, we observe that while inflation has
increased the tuition charge, the cap has kept the credit

Table 3.6. Effects of Inflation on Costs

	Enrollment (000)	Tuition	Average Credit	Cost ($000)
A. Zero elasticity, low-bound estimates[a]				
Elementary	3453	854	427	1,474,431
Secondary	1340	2162	500	670,000
Total				2,144,431
B. Elasticity-based estimates for nominal tuition				
Elementary	3722	1187	500	1,861,000
Secondary	1443	2245	500	721,500
Total				2,582,500

[a]Part A tuition is 20% larger than in Table 3.4.

at $500. Thus the real value of the subsidy declines with inflation and produces smaller enrollments in Table 3.6,B, relative to Table 3.4,B.

The logic of the economic model is also revealed by comparing tuition in A which is exactly 20 percent larger in Table 3.6 than in Table 3.4, and tuition in B, where the increase is less than the full 20 percent. Just as the elasticity-based calculations have consistently shared the benefits of the credit between parents and the school (by allowing schools to increase tuition while the net payment of parents declined), the calculations now find the schools sharing in the inflationary erosion of the value of the $500 credit. If inflation is 20 percent but tuition rises by less than 20 percent, real tuition has dropped; thus schools do share part of the loss in the real value of the credit. Furthermore, this must occur to retain enrollment equilibrium: when fewer students seek to enroll because of an erosion of the subsidy's value, schools are induced to provide fewer places through a compensating erosion in their real tuition.

In short, in an inflationary era a limit on the size of credits causes their real value to decrease; this makes intuitive sense. But the erosion of the value of the capped credit also causes enrollment to fall, reducing the number of students claiming the credit and thereby causing the federal revenue loss to decline. This decline is in both real terms (an expected result) and nominal dollar terms (possibly an unexpected result).

This logic of the inflationary process need not dictate the results; it should lead one to the conclusion that beneficiaries of the tax credit will seek to raise the limits on credits.

GENERALIZING THE RESULTS

The specific illustrations of this chapter are based on a much more general theory (see the formalized model in the appendix to this chapter). The following generalizations have emerged:

1. Even small demand elasticities of the magnitudes estimated in chapter 2 and utilized in this chapter produce estimates of revenue losses associated with tuition tax credits that are substantially larger than revenue-

loss estimates produced by zero demand elasticity
methods.

2. Maximum discrepancy between zero elasticity and
elasticity-based estimates of revenue loss occurs when the
tax credit is uncapped; the discrepancy between the two
is progressively narrowed by more restrictive maximum
limits.

3. If the tuition paid by parents is closer in
magnitude to the broad tuition than to the nominal tuition, the potential for zero elasticity estimates to
understate the true revenue loss is even greater for uncapped tuition credits (low limits on the credit reduce
this bias).

4. Even from the perspective of beneficiary
families, the tuition tax credit is somewhat regressive
in both zero elasticity and elasticity based estimates.

5. Empirically, for elementary schools only,
elasticity based estimates show the tuition tax credit
to be more regressive in its benefit distribution than
zero elasticity estimates.

6. A refundable tuition credit of 50 percent with
a $500 cap in the mid-1980s would cost about $2.6 billion
per year in lost revenue; the 1983 Reagan proposal would
cost about $1.1 billion to $1.2 billion despite its low
limit, phaseout and nonrefundability.

7. If states implement their own tuition tax
credits, the federal revenue loss would tend to be increased due to the enrollment effect.

8. In an inflationary environment, the total
revenue loss of a capped tuition tax credit will actually
decline in both nominal and real dollars, if all else is
equal, once the cap has been hit.

CONCLUSION
        The case studies presented in this chapter are
specific to the type of credit assumed, the elasticity
values used, and the underlying tuition and enrollment
figures. Yet, these calculations should not therefore
be discounted. The types of credits assumed are of the
kind that has the highest probability of enactment; and
the elasticity figures are the result of the empirical
work for 1976-1978, fairly recent years. Furthermore,
these elasticity estimates are relatively conservative
in the revenue loss estimates they produce (i.e., larger

demand elasticities would produce larger revenue loss
figures, given the supply elasticities). The enrollment
and tuition figures are both based on actual empirical
results, primarily the 1978 CPS survey.

APPENDIX TO CHAPTER 3

DERIVATION OF THE IMPACT OF A TAX CREDIT
  Using the notation of chapter 2, write

$$E_D = -a(T - C) + \text{other variables}$$

$$E_S = bT + \text{other variables}$$

where E_S and E_D are enrollment supply and demand (assumed
equal in equilibrium), T is tuition, C is dollar value of
the credit, and other variables (important in estimating
regressions) are not of importance here. Assuming equilibrium, set the right-hand sides of the equations equal
to one another and solve for T in terms of C and other
variables:

$$T = \frac{aC}{b + a} + \frac{\text{other variables}}{b + a}$$

Differentiating T with respect to C gives

$$\frac{dT}{dC} = \frac{a}{a + b}$$

Multiplying both numerator and denominator by the ratio
of tuition to enrollment converts it to

$$\frac{dT}{dC} = \frac{-e_d}{-e_d + e_s} \equiv M$$

where e_d and e_s are demand and supply elasticities. Thus
$dT = M \, dC$.
  Before proceeding further, we need to define the
following (most of which were previously encountered in
Fig. 3.1):

T_0 = equilibrium level of (nominal) tuition prior to
    credit enactment

T_1 = equilibrium tuition following enactment

E_0 = equilibrium private enrollment prior to credit enactment

E_1 = equilbrium enrollment following enactment

dT = $T_1 - T_0$, or MdC (see above), the increment in tuition caused by the credit

C = dollar value of the credit, which without a limit is cT_1 (c is the percentage of tuition allowed for the credit)

dC = incremental change in the value of the credit (dC equals C when prior to enactment of the credit the dollar value of the credit was zero)

O_0 = per pupil donations received in lieu of tuition in precredit era

T_0^* = broad definition of tuition, $T_0 + O_0$

Case I: A Simple, Unlimited Percentage Credit

If a private education market is in equilibrium with tuition T_0, we wish to find T_1 relative to T_0, given a new tax credit C. By definition,

$$T_1 = T_0 + dT = T_0 + M \, dC = T_0 + MC = T_0 + McT_1$$

where we have sequentially made substitutions from our list of definitions. If $T_1 = T_0 + McT_1$,

$$T_1 = \frac{T_0}{1 - Mc}$$

In all cases where the credit C does not exceed its limit, T_1 is found by this formula.

Case II: Credit at Maximum Limit

If cT_1 exceeds the maximum limit of the tax credit, we exploit the fact that

$$T_1 = T_0 + MC$$

where C is set at the maximum value of the credit.

Case III: Credit with Broad Definition of Tuition

Recall that the broad concept of tuition includes nominal tuition plus other payments hypothesized to be made by parents in lieu of additional tuition:

$$T_0^* = T_0 + O_0$$

If the payments in lieu of tuition are made as donations to the school in order to obtain a tax deduction, parents are receiving a tax deduction worth tO_0, where t is the tax bracket of the parents.

If one assumes that the rate of a new tax credit c is larger than most parents' tax bracket t, it is advantageous for parents to cease making donations and to incorporate such payments into tuition itself. Analyzing the impact of a newly enacted tax credit therefore requires a two-step procedure. First, parents must give up a small tax deduction worth tO_0. Then they gain tax credit. It is necessary, therefore, to define the hypothetical level of broad tuition that would prevail in the absence of both the credit and the tax deduction, T_H^*,

$$T_H^* = T_0^* - M(tO_0)$$

Once T_H^* is obtained, one may proceed as in case I or case II, with T_H^* taking the place of T_0.

Impact of Credit on Parents' Payments

In the three cases just analyzed, T_1 has been derived. The difference between T_1 and T_0 or T_0^* is the increment gained by the school. As should be apparent, $T_1 - T_0$ will not in general be equal in value to the full credit C.

After the credit is in effect, parents' net payment for private education drops to $T_1 - C$. For an uncapped credit, $T_1 - C = 0.5T_1$. But for a capped credit, the actual dollar reduction accruing to parents is the old tuition level minus the new net level of payments, or $T_0 - (T_1 - C)$. In the case of the broad tuition definition it is $(T_0^* - tO_0) - (T_1 - C)$.

Impact on Enrollment

In the previous section, the dollar increments in tuition received by the schools and the dollar reductions accruing to parents have been defined. These may be converted to percentages, and multiplied by the elasticity of supply and of demand, respectively, to give the percentage changes in enrollment that will be induced.

NOTES

1.   Martha J. Jacobs, "Tuition Tax Credits for Elementary and Secondary Education: Some Evidence," *J. Ed. Finance* 5:233-245.
2.   In the elementary sector, part B reveals that of an average credit of $267, $178 ($534 - $356) is captured by the schools through induced tuition increases; in the secondary sector, only $82 ($983 - $901) of a $491 credit is captured by the schools. In part A, no tuition changes can be induced under zero demand elasticity conditions.
3.   Technically, under the tax laws of the United States, "donations" made in the expectation of receiving a tangible benefit in return are not tax deductible (see chapter 2, note 7).
4.   Note that even though this statement in the text is meaningful, it is not the conventional measure of tax regressivity. A measure of regressivity closer to the conventional would compare the low-income students' share of benefits to low-income students' share of total (not just private) school enrollment. By such a measure, the credit is far more regressive. See Donald Frey, in *Family Choice in Schooling*, ed. M. Manley-Casimir (Lexington, Mass.: Heath, 1982).
5.   However, the absolute number of low-income students in private schools would rise, as would the dollar amount of credit benefits they receive; only the shares drop.
6.   While these figures are easy to comprehend, they understate the true tendency to direct benefits away from low-income students. According to the statement in the text, those low-income students who attend private elementary schools receive 76.7 percent of the benefit received by the typical private student. But this ignores the fact that the incidence of private-school attendance is far lower among low-income students than among others. If we restate the issue and ask what is the average credit benefit received by all low-income elementary students (public and private) relative to the national

average benefit, the ratio is only 42 percent; at the secondary level, for this tuition plan, it is only 36 percent (see Frey, ibid.).

    7. Enrollment figures from *Private Schools in American Education* (Washington, D.C.: Nat. Center Ed. Stat., 1981), Table J, were linearly extrapolated. Students in K-12 schools are assigned to elementary and secondary status in the ratio 3:1.

    8. Differences in the 1978 enrollment figures and the assumed 1985 enrollments make intertabular comparisons difficult. However, the remainder of the analysis of Table 3.4 is restricted to comparisons within the table.

    9. Enrollment by income group in 1979 found in Current Population Reports (U.S. Bureau of the Census), Series P-23, No. 121, Table 4.

    10. A comparison of the secondary sector results of part A in Tables 3.4 and 3.6 reveals some of the inherent weakness of a zero elasticity assumption. The $500 subsidy by assumption is worth 20 percent less in real terms in Table 3.6 than in Table 3.4, but the reduction in the real value of the subsidy has no effect on enrollment. Stated another way: the real value of total tuition is the same because tuition inflates by 20 percent along with the price level, but the subsidy does not inflate, so the real value of the net payment of parents (tuition minus credit) rises. However, under zero elasticity conditions, enrollment is unchanged.

CHAPTER 4

Credit Impacts on
Racial Composition and Segregation

ISSUES AND CONCEPTS

A tuition tax credit has the potential of changing the racial composition of enrollment in both public and private schools. Opponents of the credit have observed that its enactment would cause the loss of white and more affluent students from public schools--particularly urban public systems--and increase minority concentration. Advocates of the credit have made what appears to be almost the opposite claim: a credit would permit more families of modest means, including minority families, to enroll in private schools, thereby increasing the minority presence.

It is possible that both opponents and advocates are correct--the credit might increase minority proportions in both sectors simultaneously as illustrated in Table 4.1. Part A shows how a hypothetical population of 100 students, including minority students, is divided between public and private sectors of a community prior to enactment of a tax credit. Part B shows how the same 100 students might be distributed following enactment of the credit so that the minority proportions of both sectors have risen, assuming that the credit induces ten students to switch from public to private school, two are minority students, the total

Table 4.1. Racial Composition of Public and Private Enrollment

	Number White	Number Minority	Total Students	Minority Proportion	Between-sector Segregation Index
A. Before credit					
Public Schools	54	36	90	.40	.035
Nonpublic Schools	9	1	10	.10	
Total	63	37	100	.37	
B. After Credit					
Public	46	34	80	.425	.052
Nonpublic	17	3	20	.15	
Total	63	37	100	.37	

number remains at 100, and the total number of minority
students remains at 37.

    This ability of the tuition tax credit to induce an
increase in minority concentration in both sectors simultaneously is not a curiosity; it represents the fundamental mathematics of enrollment switching. The phenomenon
illustrated happens whenever public schools initially have
a minority student proportion higher than the private
schools in the same area and the proportion of minority
students induced to switch is intermediate between the two.
The first of these conditions generally holds in urban
school systems; the second condition is at least feasible.[1]

Racial Concentration and Segregation

    The proportion of minority students in public schools
versus the proportion in private schools can be shown to be
related to the degree of segregation of a community's
schools. The segregation index, which is a major measure
of segregation, is defined as

$$S = \frac{\Sigma \ E_i R_i^2}{R_{max}} \tag{4.1}$$

where the subscript i refers to the ith school in a community (whether public or private), R_i is the difference between the minority proportions in the ith school and in
all of the community's schools, E_i is the total enrollment
of the ith school. The maximum value that the numerator
may take is defined to be R_{max}; therefore, S may take values from zero to one.[2] If each school has a minority proportion equal to the communitywide minority proportion,
all the R_i^2 are zero and S is zero. The numerator would
reach its maximum value if all minority students were iso-
lated in some schools. Note that because the R_i are
squared, S puts a greater weight on large deviations from
overall racial proportions; and because each school is
weighted by its enrollment, larger schools contribute more
to the overall level of segregation. Equation (4.1) is a
crude instrument for thinking about segregation in education; to improve it, suppose that the schools of a community are divided into public and nonpublic sectors. Then
for any public school i, R_i can be broken down as

$$R_i = R_p + R_{pi} \tag{4.2}$$

where R_p is the difference between minority proportions in the entire public sector and in the entire community and R_{pi} is the difference between minority proportions in school i and in the entire public sector. Similarly, for every nonpublic school j, one can say that

$$R_j = R_n + R_{nj} \qquad (4.3)$$

where R_n is the difference between the minority proportions in the entire nonpublic sector and in the entire community and R_{nj} is the difference between the proportions in school j and in the entire nonpublic sector. Obviously, R_p is the same for every public school and R_n is the same for every nonpublic school.

Substituting (4.2) and (4.3) into (4.1) converts the communitywide segregation index into

$$S = \frac{\Sigma\ E_i R_{pi}^2 + \Sigma\ E_j R_{nj}^2 + (R_p^2 E_p + R_n^2 E_n)}{R_{max}} \qquad (4.4)$$

where E_p is the total public-sector enrollment and E_n is the total nonpublic enrollment. Expression (4.4) divides the overall segregation measure into segregation within the public sector (left term in numerator), within the nonpublic sector (middle term), and between sectors (right-hand parentheses). This separation of overall segregation into within-sector and between-sector components reveals some novel possibilities. For example, if the minority proportion of each sector deviates significantly from the overall community average, it is conceptually possible for within-sector segregation to be zero for both sectors and for between-sector segregation to be high. Conversely, the two sectors may each enroll minority students in exactly the same proportion as minorities in the overall community, thereby eliminating between-sector segregation; but individual schools within each sector may deviate greatly in minority proportions, thus creating a high level of within-sector segregation. Segregation within the public sector has been the traditional focus of federal policy; but in 1981 James Coleman et al. raised both private-sector and between-sector segregation as issues in public dialogue, although data on private-sector segregation remain scarce.[3]

The illustration of Table 4.1 is helpful here. Ignoring within-sector segregation, one finds that there is nevertheless between-sector segregation of .035 on the index for A and of .052 for B, a small but noticeable increase. Segregation increased because the switching of students from public to private sectors caused the minority proportion of the public sector to increase, and because the enrollment weighting of the sector that is more representative of the whole community (i.e., the public) declined while the enrollment weighting of the less representative sector (i.e., private) increased. Tending to offset this was the enrollment shift that made the private sector considerably more representative of the whole community than before; however, the net effect was the recorded increase in between-sector segregation.

STATISTICS ON RACIAL COMPOSITION OF ENROLLMENT

Few sources portray a complete and current picture of the racial composition of public and private enrollment. The U.S. Census Bureau's annual October Current Population Survey asks education-related questions of about 55,000 households and produces reliable estimates of public and nonpublic enrollment by race for the whole United States; however, the sample is not large enough to permit accurate estimates for most smaller political jurisdictions. The results of the Current Population Survey for 1971 and 1978 (Table 4.2) reveal that minorities constituted a higher proportion of both public and private enrollments in central cities than elsewhere. Minority students were a larger proportion of enrollment in public than in nonpublic schools everywhere—especially in central-city

Table 4.2. Racial Composition by Proportion in Metropolitan Area: (K-12)

	Central City	Other Metropolitan	Nonmetropolitan
Public, 1971			
White	.641	.920	.874
Black	.343	.065	.115
Private, 1971			
White	.896	.966	.965
Black	.086	.027	.027
Public, 1978			
White	.611	.905	.860
Black	.358	.074	.123
Hispanic	(.19)		
Private, 1978			
White	.857	.955	.983
Black	.112	.033	...
Hispanic	(.086)		

Source: Current Population Reports (U.S. Bureau of the Census) Series P-20, nos. 241, 346, Table 3 (adapted).

Note: In U.S. Census usage, Hispanics are not considered a racial group, so members of Spanish or Mexican groups appear also as members of either white or black racial groups. Proportions for white and black racial groups do not sum to 1.00 due to omission of other racial groups.

areas. Although the black enrollment of central-city private schools rose between 1971 and 1978, black enrollment remained very low relative to central-city public schools.

The nature of the Current Population Survey prevents estimations of racial composition for particular cities; and no other satisfactory annual data exist. The three-year survey of private schools undertaken by the National Center for Education Statistics between 1976-1977 and 1978-1979 did not ask about the racial or ethnic background of students.

Table 4.3 exhibits data collated from two sources for sixteen cities giving private enrollment as a percentage of public enrollment and proportions of white, black, and Hispanic students in public and nonpublic sectors. The cities represent those for which comparable public and private data were available, which explains the absence of some large cities from the list. Unlike the census data, which counts Hispanics as members of either white or black racial groups, the data in Table 4.3 count Hispanics separately, explaining why whites are generally a smaller proportion of enrollment in the cities data of Table 4.3 than in the CPS data of Table 4.2.

Although the data in Table 4.3 are too extensive to summarize completely, a few generalizations may be hazarded. In most of these cities, white enrollment in public schools is less than 50 percent; in several, blacks alone represent

Table 4.3. Segregation of Public and Private Sectors in 16 Large Cities

	Nonpublic Enrollment (% of Public Enrollment)	Nonpublic (1971)			Public (1976)			Between-Sector Contribution to Segregation[a]
		% White	% Black	% Hispanic	% White	% Black	% Hispanic	
New York	31.7	79.4	7.6	12.2	30.5	37.9	29.0	.179
Chicago	32.4	75.5	16.1	7.6	24.7	59.6	14.1	.205
Detroit	25.0	86.4	11.1	2.0	18.6	79.3	1.7	.337
Houston	8.5	80.2	6.9	12.6	34.4	42.8	23.0	.064
Baltimore	17.1	87.3	11.5	0.6	24.3	75.0	0.1	.222
Dallas	9.4	81.7	7.4	10.6	38.1	46.7	14.2	.061
Washington, D.C.	15.1	55.0	41.2	2.8	3.5	95.1	0.8	.330
Memphis	9.2	93.9	6.1	...	29.4	70.6	...	.141
San Diego	8.2	75.4	6.1	15.4	65.8	14.6	14.0	.003
Cleveland	47.5	93.6	5.2	1.1	38.5	58.2	2.8	.269
Milwaukee	35.3	95.4	3.0	1.4	56.3	37.5	4.6	.132
New Orleans	37.8	74.1	23.1	2.7	16.5	80.3	1.8	.302
Indianapolis	20.1	90.0	8.3	0.8	53.9	45.6	0.3	.076
San Francisco	30.5	67.3	8.2	16.0	27.6	29.1	14.0	.121
San Antonio	23.1	48.3	1.9	49.5	14.8	15.8	69.0	.103
Boston	31.5	91.8	5.5	2.3	44.0	42.6	9.9	.168

Source: Cols. 1-4, Diane B. Gertler, *Nonpublic Schools in Large Cities, 1970-71* (Washington, D.C.: Nat. Center for Edu. Stat., 1974), 5, Tables 2, 3 (adapted). Cols. 5-7, Report on the 100 Largest School Districts, Preliminary 1976 OS/CR Survey File (Washington, D.C.: Office for Civil Rights, n.d.)(adapted).

[a]For calculating segregation index, the minority proportion = 100% - white % in that sector. Communitywide minority proportion = weighted ave. of minority proportions for both sectors.

a clear majority of public enrollment. Hispanic enrollment is especially significant in the Southwest and New
York. Except for San Antonio, white enrollment is clearly
the majority in the nonpublic schools. In a number of
cities the private sector enrolls a substantial proportion
of black or Hispanic children, although a much smaller proportion than are enrolled in the public schools of the
same city. Finally, except for some cities in the South
and Southwest, the nonpublic enrollment is a significant
percentage of the public enrollment, commonly one-fourth
to one-third of the public enrollment.

        The right-hand column in Table 4.3 is the between-
sector segregation index, which can be calculated from the
data given in the first seven columns; however, the data
are insufficient to calculate a complete segregation index.
Using 1971 data for the private sector and 1976 data for
the public sector in calculating this column probably im-
parts a small upward bias to the index number.[4] It reveals that the between-sector component of segregation can
vary greatly, from approximately zero to approximately one-
third. Relative to the mean value of the index (.170),
cities with far below-average degrees of between-sector
segregation tend to have relatively small private sectors
(although Indianapolis is an exception); as a group, these
cities have public sectors with larger proportions of white
enrollment than other cities on the list. Cities with only
slightly less than average segregation do not, except for
Memphis, have unusually small private sectors. The reason
for below-average segregation in San Francisco and San
Antonio seems to be that their nonpublic schools have a
far higher minority proportion of enrollment, than most
other cities. The success for Milwaukee in staying below
average seems to be that the proportion of minority students in public schools is low, keeping the gap between
public and nonpublic sectors smaller than in most cities.
Finally, the cities with the largest segregation between
sectors have the largest nonpublic sectors, except for
Washington, and very high minority concentrations in the
public schools.

MODEL OF RACIAL COMPOSITION CHANGES IN ENROLLMENT
        So far the discussion has been purely descriptive,
with no behavioral hypotheses as to how a tuition tax credit might affect the racial composition of enrollment and

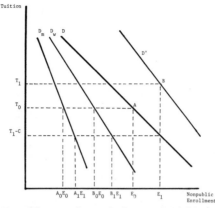

Fig. 4.1. Enrollment demand for nonpublic education by race as a function of tuition.

the index of segregation. An economic model is portrayed in Fig. 4.1. The overall demand curve for private education D is displaced to D' by the tuition tax credit (consistent with Fig. 3.1); this displacement raises overall enrollment demand from E_0 to E_1, following the analysis of chapter 3. However, Fig. 4.1 goes beyond Fig. 3.1 by representing D as the horizontal summation of the aggregate demand by whites D_w and minorities D_m. The minority demand curve lies to the left of D_w to indicate that fewer minority than white pupils will enroll. When equilibrium aggregate enrollment is E_0, the minority enrollment may be represented by A_0E_0 and the white enrollment by B_0E_0 (A_0 and B_0 are the fractions of total enrollment E_0 that minority and white students, respectively, represent; they sum to one).

Following enactment of the tax credit, tuition rises from T_0 to T_1, but parents' net payments decline to $T_1 - C$. (For clarity the supply curve is not shown in Fig. 4.1.) The aggregate enrollment of E_1 can now be divided into a minority enrollment A_1E_1 and a white enrollment of B_1E_1. There is no theoretical reason to believe that $A_0 = A_1$ or $B_0 = B_1$; some advocates of the tuition tax credit advance the argument that a credit is desirable because it would result in A_1 being greater than A_0.

The key to understanding the impact of a credit on the racial composition of public and private enrollment is the mobile group of students who switch. In Fig. 4.1, the number of minority switchers is represented by $A_1E_1 - A_0E_0$

and the number of white switchers is $B_1E_1 - B_0E_0$. Furthermore

$$A_1E_1 - A_0E_0 = e_m t A_0 E_0 \qquad (4.5)$$

$$B_1E_1 - B_0E_0 = e_w t B_0 E_0 \qquad (4.6)$$

That is, the number of switchers is equal to the respective enrollment demand elasticities (e_m = minority demand elasticity and e_w = white demand elasticity) multiplied by t (percentage drop in net tuition payments of parents) multiplied by the respective precredit enrollments of minorities and whites in the nonpublic schools.[5] The minority proportion among the total group of switching students would be (4.5) divided by the sum of (4.5) and (4.6), or

$$\frac{e_m t A_0 E_0}{e_w t B_0 E_0 + e_m t A_0 E_0} = \frac{A_0}{A_0 + (e_w/e_m)B_0} \qquad (4.7)$$

Since $A_0 + B_0 = 1$, (4.7) collapses to A_0 if $e_w = e_m$. That is, when the demand elasticities of enrollment are the same for both race groups, the minority proportion of switching students will be exactly the same as the minority proportion A_0 already in the private sector. Expression (4.7) reveals that only if e_m is larger than e_w (more negative) will the minority proportion of the group switching into private schools be greater than the minority proportion of the group already there; and only if this happens can a tax credit increase minority proportions in the private sector.

What Happens in the Public Sector?

Figure 4.1 is cast in terms of nonpublic enrollment patterns, which is compatible with the analysis of chapters 2 and 3. However, with a few modifications the model can be used to formalize how public-sector racial composition is affected by a tax credit. It is necessary to define some terms that are the public equivalents to the private sector variables A, B, and E. Let P_0 and P_1 be total public-sector enrollment prior to and after a tuition tax credit, H_0 and H_1 be the fraction of minority public students prior to and after a tuition tax credit, and the ratio E_0/P_0 be nonpublic enrollment as a proportion of public enrollment prior to the credit. Given these definitions, the total number of public-school minority students prior to a credit is $H_0 P_0$. Subtracting the number of minority switchers given by (4.6) from $H_0 P_0$ gives the number of minority students left in the public sector after the credit has gone into effect. Dividing this by total public enrollment prior to the credit P_0 minus all switchers gives H_1, the proportion of minority students left in the public schools after a tuition tax credit:

$$H_1 = \frac{H_0 P_0 - e_m t A_0 E_0}{P_0 - (e_w B_0 + e_m A_0) t E_0} = \frac{H_0 - e_m t A_0 (E_0/P_0)}{1 - (e_w B_0 + e_m A_0) t (E_0/P_0)}$$

$$(4.8)$$

The right-hand side of (4.8) is obtained by dividing both numerator and denominator by the reciprocal of P_0; this makes it possible to deal exclusively with private enrollment as a proportion of public enrollment rather than with absolute enrollment figures, which is far easier.

IMPACT ON RACIAL ENROLLMENT PATTERNS

Equation (4.8) may be exploited to estimate the likely impact of a tuition tax credit on the racial enrollment pattern of a hypothetical city having the characteristics described by the Current Population Survey for 1978 (Table 4.2). Specifically, this statistically typical city would have a minority enrollment of 40 percent in the public sector and 15 percent in the private sector; total private enrollment would be about 25 percent of the total public enrollment. Let us assume, further, that behavioral patterns would reflect the results of chapter 2: the demand elasticity for private education of white students would be -0.4.

Chapter 2 presents evidence that the demand elasticity of lower income students in elementary schools is less than the overall demand elasticity. However, this result was not explicitly derived from data on minority students, and it would seem unwise to assume a particular value e_m. Therefore, a range of values for e_m, from -0.2 to -0.8, will be assumed.

Chapter 3 demonstrates that a 50 percent tuition tax credit could reduce the net payments of parents anywhere from zero (if the supply elasticity is zero) to a full 50 percent (if the supply elasticity is infinite). Therefore,

Table 4.4. Impact of Credit on Public and Private Enrollments: Hypothetical City

Reduction of Parents' Payments (%)	Demand Elasticity of Minority Students (e_m) (majority elasticity set at -0.4)			
	-0.2	-0.3	-0.4	-.08
A. Minority % in public schools after credit (40% before credit)				
0	40.0	40.0	40.0	40.0
-30	40.9	40.8	40.7	40.5
-50	41.5	41.4	41.3	40.8
B. Minority % in private schools after credit (15% before credit)				
0	15.0	15.0	15.0	15.0
-30	14.3	14.7	15.0	16.4
-50	14.1	14.5	15.0	17.2
C. Private enrollment as % of public enrollment after credit (25% before credit)				
0	25.0	25.0	25.0	25.0
-30	28.6	28.7	28.9	29.5
-50	31.1	31.3	31.6	32.6
D. Between-sector segregation index after credit (0.044 before credit)				
0	.044	.044	.044	.044
-30	.054	.052	.050	.045
-50	.060	.058	.056	.045

Note: The hypothetical city's educational system approximates the aggregate U.S. results for central cities: initially public minority enrollment = 40%, private = 15%, and private enrollment is assumed to be 25% of public enrollment.

a range of possible reductions in parental net payments is assumed; a 30 percent reduction is a reasonable average experienced by both elementary and secondary parents.

Table 4.4 shows the projected effects of a tuition tax credit on racial enrollment patterns in the hypothetical typical city for several combinations of assumptions. Part A shows the projected minority percent of enrollment in the public schools after enactment of the credit. The first row illustrates that if the tuition tax credit fails to reduce parental net payments (because the schools manage to capture the full impact) there can be no impact at all on enrollment; minority concentration will remain exactly at 40 percent. The rest of A produces two conclusions under the set of assumptions chosen: (1) The tuition tax credit increases minority concentration in the public sector; and (2) the increase is small.

A general rule is that the larger the reductions in parents' payments, the larger the enrollment switching and the larger the increase of the minority percentage in the public schools. A second generalization is that the smaller the assumed demand elasticity of minorities relative to whites, the greater the increase in minority concentration in the public sector as the result of the credit. Part A also demonstrates that a minority demand elasticity greater than that of the majority (-0.8, for example) does not guarantee that the minority concentration in the public sector will not increase due to a tax credit.[6] While it

is possible for minority demand elasticity to be large
enough for a tax credit to reduce minority percentages in
the public schools, the size of such a demand elasticity
seems much larger than is likely to exist. (Note that -0.8
is twice as large as the assumed majority elasticity of
-0.4, and A still shows minority concentration increasing
as a result of the tax credit.)

Part A, in short, confirms the claims of opponents
of tuition tax credits in a qualitative sense: the minority concentration in public schools does increase according to the model. However, the size of the impact seems
small. The largest minority percentage is barely 42 percent, hardly a large increase over the initial 40 percent.

Part B shows the impact of the credit on minority
concentration in the private sector. Part B confirms that
if minority and majority demand elasticities are the same
(-0.4), then the minority percentage in the private sector
will not be changed by the credit because the minority proportion among the students induced to switch by the credit
will just equal the proportion already attending private
schools. If the minority elasticity is less than that of
the majority (closer to zero than -0.4), the credit reduces
minority proportions in the private schools, and vice versa.
As with A, B shows that any changes are likely to be small;
the largest change in the minority percentage in private
schools is only about 2 points. The right-hand columns
in A and B illustrate the apparent paradox discussed earlier in this chapter: minority percentages are capable
of rising simultaneously in both public and private sectors.

Part C reveals how the tax credit would increase
private enrollments relative to public enrollments (provided the supply elasticity and thus t are not zero). As
should be expected, a greater gain in the private sector
reflects a greater reduction in net payments and a greater
minority demand elasticity. Here one finds somewhat larger
changes than in A and B; the largest illustrated impact of
the credit would push private enrollment from about one-
fourth to about one-third of public enrollment.

Finally, part D shows the between-sector index of
segregation for the hypothetical city. The between-sector
index was .044 prior to enactment of the credit; all the
new values of the index are not much larger. The increase
in the segregation index in proportionate terms is large
in some cases, but this is a reflection of the small ini-

tial value of the index rather than the size of any of the
increases. Part D cannot show how a tuition tax credit
might affect segregation within either sector, however.

To summarize the results of Table 4.4, for parts
A, B, and D the results are all tightly clustered. Despite
a large number of combinations of assumed values of minority demand elasticities and net reductions in parents' payments, the outcomes seem to be rather homogeneous; while
the credit increases both minority concentration in the
public sector and between-sector segregation, these effects are small. In addition, while the credit might con-
ceivably increase or decrease minority proportions in the
private sector, the effect again seems small. Only in C
does one find large effects; under most favorable assumptions private enrollment relative to public could potentially grow from one-fourth to about one-third.

A Worst-Case Estimate for Between-Sector Segregation

It is possible that the relatively benign results
shown by Table 4.4 depend heavily on the precredit enrollment profile of the hypothetical city. Equation (4.8)
shows that a credit would increase minority concentration
in public schools more when (1) the initial minority concentration in the public sector is larger, (2) the minority concentration in the private sector is smaller, and
(3) the private sector is proportionately larger. Therefore, let us examine a city with much more extreme enrollment characteristics than the hypothetical city of Table
4.4.

Detroit in the mid-1970s possessed most of the characteristics that would allow a tuition tax credit to have
its maximum impact on racial concentration and segregation.
In order to maximize the likely tax credit impact, Table
4.5 is calculated with a minority demand elasticity assumed
to be only − 0.3 and with the impact of the credit on net
payments of parents assumed to be a full 50 percent.

The table reveals that under these assumptions minority concentration in the public schools rises from 81.0 to

Table 4.5. Maximum Impact of a Credit on Minority Enrollments, Private Enrollments, and Segregation in Detroit: Early 1970s

	Minority Enrollment (%)		Private Enrollment (% of Public Enrollment)	Between-Sector Segregation Index
	Public	Private		
Before credit	81.0	14.0	25.0	.328
After credit	84.6	13.6	31.3	.420
Change, %	4.4	−2.9	25.3	28.000

Table assumes that credit reduces parents' net payments t by 50%, $e_w = -0.4$, and $e_m = -0.3$.

84.6 percent, while the minority percentage in private
schools drops marginally. Meanwhile, total private enrollment rises from 25 to 31.3 percent of public enrollment, a
relatively large gain. The between-sector segregation index rises from .328 to .420, a moderately large increase
in both absolute and proportionate terms. This increase
in the segregation index reflects three contributory ele-
ments: the public and private minority proportions are
each further from the communitywide minority proportion
after the credit-induced enrollment shifts; and the private sector, whose minority proportion is further from the
communitywide proportion, receives a heavier weighting
after the credit is in effect.

The conclusion is that the opponents of the tuition
tax credit are correct in a qualitative sense: the credit
should be expected to increase the minority racial concentration of the public schools and to increase between-
sector segregation. The magnitude of the effect, in absolute terms however, does not appear to be very large--al-
though what constitutes "large" may vary depending on the
observer.

RACIAL CONCENTRATION AND SEGREGATION WITHIN
THE PUBLIC SECTOR
Federal policy in education has not been concerned
with minority concentration per se, but with segregation
and not so much with between-sector segregation as with
segregation within the public sector. Might there be a
link between increased minority concentration in the public sector (which is likely to occur with a tax credit)
and increased segregation within the public sector?

There is no purely logical reason why increased minority proportions in the public schools should necessarily make segregation worse. In theory, school administrators
might ensure the minority students were spread equiproportionately across all the schools of a district, no
matter how small or large the overall concentration of
minority students in the system. Yet integration of the
public schools, as viewed in this manner, faces many political and pragmatic obstacles. There is reason to believe that these obstacles become greater as the minority
proportion rises, especially as it rises above 50 percent.
Orfield asserts that when white enrollment drops below 50
percent of public enrollment, the will of courts to order
full integration falters.[7] Surely at some point the re-

Table 4.6. Statistics for Public-School Segregation Index Regressed on
            Minority Enrollment of Large School Districts: 1972

Region	Constant Term	Coefficient of Minority %	R^2	N	Mean Value of Segregation Index
South	.07	.0053 (3.5)	.19	56	.25
Northeast-north central	.22	.0051 (4.3)	.36	35	.49
West-southwest	.09	.0048 (4.2)	.25	54	.24

Source of data: B. S. Zoloth, "Alternative Measures of School Segregation,"
Land Economics 52(3): Appendix.
    t-values = ( )

maining white enrollment in a school system is so low that
further efforts at integration are seen as merely fulfill-
ing the letter of the law without conferring any of the
intended benefits. These speculations suggest that increasing minority concentrations may lead to increased
segregation within the public sector.

To test this hypothesis, segregation indexes for a
number of large public systems were regressed on the minority percentage of those systems. The results, by region,
are given in Table 4.6. Since the only independent variable is minority percentage, the coefficient of the minority variable reflects both direct and indirect effects
that minority concentration has on the segregation index.
Indirect effects occur when the minority concentration influences another variable that in turn influences the degree of segregation.

In all three regions the effect of increasing minority concentration in a public school district increases the
degree of segregation of the public system. The coefficients of the three regions are very similar (all close to
.005, and all highly significant). The interpretation is
that an increase in minority concentration of one percentage point would increase the segregation index by .005.
Considering that the average value of the public-school
segregation index in the South and West is about .25, this
represents 2 percent increase in the segregation index; in
the North, where the average value of the segregation index
is .49, this would represent about 1 percent increase in
segregation.

An effort was made to see if 50 percent minority concentration represented a threshold beyond which efforts to
integrate collapsed, with the segregation index rising more
in response to increases in minority concentration over 50
percent than below 50 percent. The regression results did
not confirm the existence of such a threshold.

Table 4.7. Estimated Impact of Hypothetical Tax Credit on Minority Proportion in 16 Cities: Mid-1970s[a]

City	Minority Proportion in Public Schools (% of total)		Estimated Increase in Segregation Index (%)[d]
	Precredit[b]	Estimated Postcredit[c]	
New York	69.5	71.5	1.8
Chicago	75.3	77.4	1.8
Detroit	81.4	83.5	1.7
Houston	65.6	66.1	0.6
Baltimore	75.7	77.0	1.5
Dallas	61.9	62.4	0.6
Washington, D.C.	96.5	97.5	0.9
Memphis	70.6	71.3	1.4
San Diego	34.2	34.3	0.2
Cleveland	61.5	64.9	3.2
Milwaukee	43.7	45.5	2.1
New Orleans	83.5	86.3	2.9
Indianapolis	46.1	47.0	1.0
San Francisco	72.4	74.0	1.8
San Antonio	85.2	86.1	0.9
Boston	56.0	57.9	3.7

[a]Impact of credit on minority enrollment assumes net parental payment reduced 30%; minority demand elasticity = -0.3; white demand elasticity = -0.4.

[b]Equals 100% - corresponding value in col. (5), Table 4.3.

[c]Calculated from Eq. (4.8) using values of ratios in Table 4.3 and assumptions in note a.

[d]Pre- and postcredit % substituted in equations of Table 4.6 to estimate segregation index values.

The regression equations in Table 4.6 can be used to estimate public-sector segregation indexes for the cities in Table 4.3 and to project estimates in the segregation index likely to be caused by the tax credit under moderate assumptions (Table 4.7). The change in the segregation index is estimated by substituting both precredit and post-credit minority percentages into the regression equations in Table 4.6. The conclusion from the third column of Table 4.7 fits the pattern: the qualitative effect is greater segregation; the size of the effect is small. Since these cities tend to display a pattern of enrollments more conducive to large credit-induced increases in minority concentration than found generally, one may feel safe in concluding that any credit-induced increase in public-sector segregation exceeding 5 percent is unlikely. This should not, however, minimize the fact that a tax credit is likely to push public-sector segregation in a direction contrary to stated federal policy.

ARE PRIVATE SCHOOLS AN ANSWER TO SEGREGATION?

The link that exists between minority concentration and segregation in the public sector provides a perspective on a finding by James Coleman that segregation of blacks and whites is less within the private secondary sector than within the public secondary sector.[8] One may ask whether the Coleman finding seems credible and whether such a find-

ing would justify a federal policy of promoting enrollment
in the private sector.

These regressions in Table 4.6 imply that if minority proportions were as low in the public sector as they
are in the private sector, the segregation index for the
public sector also should be low; a finding like Coleman's
would be expected if private behavior with respect to segregation did nothing but follow the behavioral patterns
found in the public sector.

An example illustrates the magnitudes involved. Suppose that a typical urban public school system has a 60
percent minority enrollment and the private schools of
the same city a 25 percent minority enrollment. Then by
the regression for the Northeast-North Central states in
Table 4.6, the predicted segregation index for the public
system is 50 percent larger than it would be if its minority enrollment were as low as in the private schools.
Using the regression equations for the South and West-South-
west, the estimated segregation is 85 percent larger than
it would be if the public minority concentration were as
low as in the private sector of the same city. In fact,
the Coleman study reports the black-white within-sector
segregation for the public schools to be about 69 percent
larger than for the private sector in its sample. A segregation differential of this magnitude is what the regressions predict. The inference to be drawn is that the
fundamental behavior of private schools with respect to
segregation is not necessarily different from that of the
public sector.

In view of this, any empirical finding that private
schools have low segregation indexes should not be trans-
formed into federal policy to encourage enrollment switching into the private sector. The lower index numbers do
not necessarily denote a greater private commitment to integration; if private enrollments were to rise, the segregation index in the private sector might well rise, too.

SUMMARY AND CONCLUSIONS

This chapter considers three aspects of segregation:
between-sector segregation, public-sector segregation, and
private-sector segregation. A constant theme is that the
degree of segregation is related to the proportion (or concentration) of minority students in the two sectors.

Between-sector segregation exists because the minor-

ity concentrations in public and private sectors differ
from the overall proportion of minority students.   Table
4.4 implies that a tax credit causing students to switch
from public to private schools would increase between-
sector segregation even if the switch causes an increase
in proportion of minority students in the private sector.
However, the table also shows that the increase in between-
sector segregation would be small.

Another clear finding is that for all plausible parameter values, a tax credit would tend to cause an increase
in the minority concentration of the public sector (even
when the minority proportion of the private sector was induced to rise also).   This becomes more significant in
light of the evidence that increasing minority concentration in the public sector tends to increase segregation in
the public sector.

These findings are consistent with the claims made
by opponents of the tuition tax credit.   However, note the
second major result of the chapter: for the wide range of
reasonable values assigned to the parameters of the calculations, almost all the effects on minority concentration
and segregation have been of a small magnitude.   Therefore,
it is likely that extreme partisans, either for or against
the tax credit, will not be happy with these results.

These results suggest that increasing private enrollment is not a good way to fight segregation even if segregation within the private sector were less than within the
public sector.   While there may be some gain to be had by
moving students to a possibly less segregated sector, it
is offset by increases in between-sector segregation, increases in public-sector segregation, and perhaps even
segregation increases within the private sector itself.

NOTES

1. The elasticities estimated in chapter 2 suggest
that low-income (and possibly, therefore, minority) students are less sensitive to tuition changes; therefore,
minority representation among students switching to private schools may well be lower than among students already
in private schools.

2. Technically $R_{max} = Er(1 - r)$, where E is total
enrollment of all schools of the community and r is the

communitywide minority proportion. This definition of the segregation index is discussed in B. S. Zoloth, "Alternative Measures of School Segregation," *Land Econ.*, 52(3).

3. James Coleman et al., *Public and Private Schools* (Chicago, Ill.: Nat. Opinion Res. Center, 1981), xxv, 49-50. This newest Coleman report claims that nonpublic high schools are better integrated for blacks than public schools (though not necessarily for Hispanics). For a methodological critique for Coleman's work, see Ellis B. Page and Timothy Z. Keith, "Effects of U.S. Private Schools: A Technical Analysis of Two Recent Claims," *Ed. Res.*, Aug./ Sept., 1981, 7-17.

4. If the trends of Table 4.2 apply to each of the cities in Table 4.3, public-school minority proportions would have been smaller in 1971 than in 1976 and nonpublic-sector minority proportions would have been larger in 1976 than in 1971. Therefore, segregation index calculations using 1971 data exclusively, or 1976 data exclusively, might have produced somewhat smaller numbers. However, any such bias should be small.

5. Just as the minority and white demand elasticities may differ, it is possible that the two groups face different net payment reductions t; however, this would be analytically similar to a different demand elasticity. Because evidence is scarce, and for simplicity, t is assumed to be the same for both groups.

6. This result is entirely in keeping with the logic of the theory developed earlier in the chapter. The demand elasticity of minorities greater (more negative) than the demand elasticity of the majority only guarantees that the minority proportion among students induced to switch from public to private sectors will exceed the minority proportion already in the private sector. Yet, the minority proportion among switchers may still be smaller than among public students, causing minorities to be a larger percentage of students left behind in the public sector.

7. Gary Orfield, *Must We Bus?* (Washington, D. C.: Brookings, 1978), 26, 27.

8. Coleman, 44, for black-white segregation indexes within sectors. See Page and Keith for a critique of Coleman's segregation index.

CHAPTER 5

Local Support
for Public Education

Public education in the United States is primarily a function of state and local governments, in which the local electorate often has a substantial say in determining levels of expenditure. If political support for public-school spending is greatest among parents of children attending public schools, then enactment of a tuition tax credit that reduces enrollment in the public sector might be expected to result in a reduction of public-sector expenditures. This chapter reviews some evidence that bears on this hypothesis.

A CONCEPTUAL FRAMEWORK

Voters without school-aged children and voters with children in private schools would--aside from any purely ethical commitment to public education--support expenditures for public education because of a perception that they benefit the community generally (*externalities*). Parents whose children attend public schools have an additional reason to support public-education expenditures--their own children benefit directly.

What level of per pupil expenditures are various types of voter-taxpayers willing to support? Suppose the voter-taxpayers receive incomes from which education taxes are deducted, and after-tax income is spent on private goods or services. The voters derive some satisfaction (*utility*) from expenditures on both private goods and public education. If the marginal utility derived from these expenditures is subject to diminishing returns, an individual's choice in allocating income between private goods and public education may be explained by Fig. 5.1. The horizon-

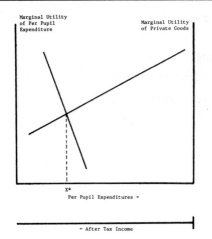

Fig. 5.1. Determination of desired per pupil expenditure.

tal axis measures per pupil levels of public-school expenditure, holding constant the number of students in the public school system. For any level of per pupil expenditure,
the taxpayer will owe a specified amount of education taxes
--higher taxes associated with higher per pupil levels of
expenditure.[1] Because of this feature, the horizontal
axis may be interpreted also as measuring after-tax income:
after-tax income is at its maximum when per pupil expenditures (thus taxes for education) are zero; it declines as
per pupil expenditure rises. Hypothetically, at some very
high level of per pupil expenditure, the taxpayer's after-
tax income could be reduced to zero. In effect, the horizontal axis shows how a taxpayer's income is divided between expenditures on public education and on private goods.
     The left vertical axis of Fig. 5.1 reflects the mar-
ginal utility of per pupil expenditures on public education. The right vertical axis (which rises from the point
on the horizontal axis where per pupil expenditures would
be so large as to reduce the taxpayer's after-tax income
to zero) indicates the marginal utility to the individual
of private goods. The figure shows that both marginal
utility curves slope down and away from their respective
vertical axes due to the assumption of diminishing returns.
The voter-taxpayer maximizes the total satisfaction (utility) possible from a given income by choosing the desired

level of per pupil, public-school expenditures X* where
the marginal utility curves intersect.[2] (This does not
imply that the political process will necessarily accom-
modate the individual by choosing X*.)

It can be shown that the height of the two curves in
the diagram depends on the total number of pupils in the
public schools. First, consider the marginal utility
curve for private goods, which reflects a particular level
of enrollment. Then, assume that enrollment in the public
system drops. With enrollment smaller, any particular per
pupil level of expenditure requires a smaller total expenditure. Therefore, the amount of education taxes needed
from each taxpayer to sustain a given per pupil expenditure drops, which implies that after-tax income is higher.
This additional income is spent on private goods, which
are subject to diminishing marginal utility. Therefore,
the marginal utility of private consumption associated
with a given level of per pupil expenditure must have
dropped and the marginal utility of private consumption
curve shifts down.[3]

If a reduction in the number of public school pupils
had only this effect, X* clearly would move to the right
as the marginal utility of private consumption dropped.
However, the marginal utility of the school expenditure
curve might shift as well. Obviously, the marginal utility received from school expenditures should drop for families whose children are leaving the public system and
causing the drop in public enrollment, and it may decline
for other voters also; the community external benefits from
public education are probably related to the number of publicly educated pupils. For example, employers who enjoy
the advantages of a literate work force receive larger benefits from public education when a higher proportion of the
work force is publicly educated. In general, the perceived
benefits to the wider community depend on citizens actually
coming in contact with publicly educated pupils. This line
of reasoning suggests that a reduction in the number of public-school pupils would cause the marginal utility curve
for public expenditure to shift down, even for those families who have no children in public school.[4]

If a reduction of enrollment in the public schools
causes both marginal utility curves to shift, the overall
effect cannot be determined by theory alone; X* could either rise or fall for any particular voter. In the aggregate, however, the direction of change is ambiguous.

Enrollment Switching and Public Expenditure

In simplest terms, a tuition tax credit induces a reduction in public school enrollment by reducing net payments required for private schooling. However, the decision faced by families considering switches to private
schools is worth examining in detail; their role is exceptionally important.

In deciding whether to enroll a child in a private
school, a family must remember that its after-tax income
will be reduced by tuition payments. A family, therefore,
will use private schools only if the utility, or satisfaction, of private education is at least as large as (1) the
utility of the public education that is otherwise freely
available plus (2) the utility of the private goods and
services that the tuition payment might otherwise have pur-
chased. Clearly the magnitude of the tuition payment plays
a key role. Further, there exists some tuition payment low
enough (possibly negative for some families) to induce almost any family to use the private schools. A tuition tax
credit would reduce the effective tuition confronting parents, and for some families (switchers) the credit would
make the payments low enough to transfer children from public to private school. Nonswitchers are families unaf-
fected by the credit: their children remain either in public or private schools despite enactment of a credit.

Enrollment switching may have a significant impact
on a family's support for public per pupil expenditures because switchers are subject to two special effects: (1)
Because a switcher's own child no longer benefits from public schooling, the switcher-voter's marginal utility curve
for public-school expenditures is subject to an exceptionally large downward shift. (2) Unlike other voters, the
switcher's marginal utility curve for private goods is subject to an upward shift; the family undertakes tuition payments, which implies that some other form of private consumption of lesser utility is displaced.[5] This upward
shift probably overwhelms any downward shifts of this
curve for a switcher-voter.[6] By reference to Fig. 5.1,
we can see that this should move X*, the desired level
of public expenditures, to the left.

This kind of analysis produces a surprising result
for one category of voter--the parents of children in private schools before enactment of a credit. These voter-
taxpayers are subject to the same influnces as nonparent
voters; however, a tuition tax credit would affect this
category of voters in a unique way. Because they have al-

ready been paying tuition, the tax credit represents an un-
ambiguous net gain in spendable income to them and the
credit gives an extra downward impetus to their marginal
utility curve for private goods. This would tend, therefore, to make this group more likely than nonparent voters
to raise their desired levels of X*--a perhaps unexpected
result.

In sum, a tuition tax credit that reduced the overall
enrollment of public schools would have an ambiguous effect
on the desired level of public, per pupil expenditures
among most voters. However, among those most directly affected by a tax credit (switchers), the likely effect is a
reduction in the desired level of per pupil public expenditures. There is also the surprising conclusion that parents of precredit private-school students may favor larger
increases in X* (or smaller decreases) as a result of a
tax credit than otherwise-similar nonparent voters.

PRIVATE ENROLLMENT AND PUBLIC EXPENDITURE:
EMPIRICAL LINK

Because no tuition tax credit has yet been enacted,
there can be no direct measurement of the effect of a credit on public expenditures. However, the reasoning of the
previous section is in terms of concepts that can be readily translated into currently observable variables. It is
possible, for example, to observe how differences in the
proportion of students enrolled in public schools across
school districts or states affects per pupil expenditures.
Even in the absence of a tuition tax credit, public enrollment as a proportion of total enrollment varies widely
across districts, which makes it possible to seek an empirical link between enrollment and support for public expenditures.

Guidelines for Surveying the Literature

A number of studies have dealt with the determinants
of public per pupil spending, and several have included
some measure of public enrollment as one of the determinants. Most of the studies are cross sectional, with an
individual school district as the unit of observation and
multiple regression analysis is used to measure the effects of a number of determinants of expenditure in addition to the one of interest. Before surveying the conclusions of these studies, we should consider some guidelines
for assessing their adequacy.

Tax-base variable. According to the model illustrated by Fig. 5.1, a change in public enrollment has an ambiguous impact on per pupil expenditure. The marginal utility curve for public expenditure drops in direct response to reduction of public enrollment; the marginal utility curve for private goods drops indirectly as lower enrollments produce a drop in taxes needed to produce a given per pupil level of expenditure. Therefore, if the regression equation explaining per pupil expenditure includes some measure of public enrollment but does not specify the tax-reduction effects of changing enrollment, the coefficient of the enrollment variable would reveal the combined effects of both marginal utility curves shifting. Let

$$X = pE + qZ \qquad\qquad (5.1)$$

where X is per pupil expenditure, E is an enrollment measure, Z is a vector of exogenous variables excluding the tax rate, and the lowercase letters are estimated coefficients. The coefficient p reveals the combined effect of incremental changes in enrollment on per pupil expenditures; the sign of p may be either positive or negative, depending on which effect dominates. However, let

$$X = p_1E + p_2B + qZ \qquad\qquad (5.2)$$

where B is the tax base per pupil (or a similar variable that would hold taxpayer's rates constant).[7] Coefficient p_1 reflects the direct impact of enrollment changes (i.e., the effect of shifting the marginal utility curve for school expenditure while the marginal utility curve for private goods is artificially held constant); coefficient p_2 shows the effect of changes in tax base per pupil on per pupil expenditures and could be used to calculate the indirect effect of a change in enrollment on per pupil expenditures.[8]

Simultaneity. Studies of the link between per pupil expenditure and public enrollment should not overlook the possibility that they are jointly determined. The better studies of the determinants of per pupil expenditures are those that compensate for the problem of simultaneous determination of variables.

Definition of enrollment. The exact definition of the en-

rollment variable is also of great interest. If public
enrollment were measured in absolute numbers, the variable
might simply be a proxy for economies or diseconomies of
scale. To avoid this problem the enrollment variable must
be some measure of per capita enrollment--e.g., public enrollment as a proportion of all children of a certain age
group or as a proportion of all students. A community-
enrollment variable stated as the proportion of all students enrolled in the public schools can be converted im-
mediately into a private-enrollment variable (for public
plus private enrollments must equal 100 percent of overall
community enrollment).

The sample. Another guideline involves the sample of
school districts used for the study. Studies of school
districts where the local political process is relatively
important in determining school expenditures are preferred
because the impact of enrollment changes on support for
public education must be greatest where local revenues subject to local control are a large proportion of total expenditures on education. Nonlocal revenues for public
schools are often allocated to school districts with no
respect for the local political process. It is also desirable that the enrollment percentages are highly variable
across the sample; this helps to protect against the possibility that the impact of enrollment changes occurs only
above some threshold.

Other variables. Per pupil expenditure equations should,
at a minimum, specify a number of other variables besides
the one(s) of primary interest; theory suggests that expenditures depend on a number of influences. Three broad
categories of control variables can be recognized: (1)
Demand variables are those that tend to influence a community's demand for high- or low-expenditure public education
and include state or federal subsidies that stimulate local
expenditures, income levels in the community, and various
proxies for a community's regard for education. (2) Supply
variables include all variables that affect the costs of
public education and include the prices of inputs (primarily wages of teachers) and scale economies. (3) Institu-
tional variables represent the legal or political struc-
tures through which educational spending decisions are made
and include collective bargaining or the elective status of
the school boards.

The Literature

     By these guidelines, the existing studies (Table 5.1)
are of mixed quality. Although all specify a variety of
demand variables, several contain no supply-side control
variables; the degree to which this might bias the results
of interest is not certain. The northeastern and midwestern states are most heavily represented, which is reasonable because private enrollments are highest there. Several of the studies did employ techniques to compensate
for the possibility that enrollment and expenditures per
pupil were jointly determined. Despite the variety in
these studies, their findings (Table 5.2), with but one
exception, are very similar.

     Because the studies defined variables in a variety of
ways and because a variety of functional forms were utilized in the regressions, the presentation of the results
in their original form would be almost imcomprehensible.
Therefore, all results are restated in a common format.
Specifically, Table 5.2 represents elasticities of public
per pupil expenditure with respect to private enrollment.
Although the calculations necessary to convert the results
to a common format are tedious, they are fairly straightforward and are not reproduced here.[9] The partial elasticity is defined as the percent change in public per pupil
expenditure per 1 percent change in private enrollment,
holding constant the per pupil tax base of the public sector; this partial elasticity registers only the direct
impact of private-school enrollment while ignoring the indirect effects caused by changes in the tax base as public
enrollments change. The combined elasticity reports the
total response of public per pupil expenditures to a 1 percent change in private enrollment. The only way to disen-
tangle the partial effect of a change in private enrollment from the combined effect is to control explicitly for
the tax base in a multiple regression; therefore for studies that did not control for the tax base, only the combined elasticity can be reported.

     The model above suggests that the partial elasticity
should be negative. It also suggests that the indirect effect of an increase in private enrollment which increases
per pupil tax base for students remaining in the public
sector, is to increase per pupil expenditure. Since the
partial (direct) effect and the indirect effect have opposite signs, the combined elasticity may be either positive
or negative.

     The results seem to bear out the first prediction.
Of 16 reported partial elasticities, 12 have negative signs,

Table 5.1. Per Pupil Expenditures: Characteristics (x indicates presence of variables in regressions)

Author[a]	Sample	Tax Base per Pupil	Nonlocal Revenue	Community Income	Socioeconomic Factors	Other Demand	Size of District (scale)	Wage Pressure	Other Supply	Collective Bargaining	District Governance	Significant Private Enrollment	Significant Local Revenues	Deals with Simultaneity of Equations
Cohn (Table 5-4)	states, 1967		x	x	x		x		x			mixed	mixed	yes
Davis (Table 7)	districts in Pa., 1958			x	x							yes	yes	no
Denzau	districts in Va., 1969	(regression variables not reported)										no	yes	no
Feldstein	districts in Mass., 1965, 1970	x	x	x		x						yes	yes	yes
Frey	districts in N.J., 1973	x	x	x			x	x	x	x		yes	yes	yes
Grubb & Osman	districts in Calif., 1971	x	x	x	x	x			x			no	yes	no
Gustman & Pidot	urban areas in U.S., 1962			x	x	x	x	x	x			yes	yes	yes
Ladd	districts in Boston SMSA, 1970	x	x	x	x	x						yes	yes	no
Lovell	districts in Conn., 1970	x	x	x		x	x		x		x	yes	yes	no
Miner	states, 1959	x	x	x	x		x	x	x		x	yes	yes	no
Miner	districts in various states, 1959			x	x						x	mixed	yes	no

[a]See references at end of chapter.

Table 5.2. Public per Pupil Expenditure Elasticities with Respect to Private Enrollment (% change in per pupil expenditure per 1% increase in private enrollment)

Author	Equation Reference	Partial Elasticity	Combined Elasticity	Underlying Coefficient Significant?
Feldstein				
(Table 1)	1.1	−1.16	−1.10	yes
	1.2	−1.22	−1.17	no
	1.3	−0.16	−0.11	no
	1.4	+1.13	1.18	no
	1.5	−0.16	−0.14	no
	1.8[a]	−1.57	−1.49	no
Frey				
(Appendix)	1	−0.05	−0.03	yes
	2	−0.07	−0.04	no
Grubb & Osman				
(Table 2)[b]	1	−0.04	−0.03	yes
	2	0.00	+0.03	yes
	3	0.00	+0.03	no
	4	+0.05	+0.06	mixed
Ladd	1	−0.01	+0.04	no
	2	−0.03	+0.04	no
	3	−0.03	+0.04	no
Lovell				
(Table 2)	4	−0.01	+0.01	no
Cohn				
(Table 5-4)	2a		−0.01	no
	2b		+0.22	no
Davis				
(Table 7)	1		+0.15	yes
Denzau	3		+0.04	yes
(Table 3)	5		+0.03	yes
	11		+0.04	yes
	13		+0.05	yes
Gustman & Pidot				
(Table 1)			+0.15	yes
Miner				
(Table 1)	U.S.		+0.02	no
(Table 11)	Ill.		−0.04	no
	Mich.		+0.01	no
	N.J.		+0.05	no
	N.Y.		−0.03	no
(Table 15)	Conn.		−0.07	no
	Mass.		+0.11	yes

Sources: See references at end of chapter.

[a]Feldstein regressions (1.6) and (1.7) constrain coefficients so that no independent estimate of the combined elasticity is possible.

[b]Grubb and Osman (Table 1) results omitted because their table and text are apparently contradictory.

only 2 are positive, and 2 are approximately zero. Except for 4 deduced from the Feldstein study, all the reported elasticities are very small. Since the Feldstein results are highly variable, both in magnitude and in sign and since their magnitudes are unlike those of any of the other studies, these results are discounted in the remainder of the chapter.

Of 31 reported combined elasticities, 12 are nega-

tive and 19 positive. This division of signs suggests
that neither the direct nor the indirect effect predomi-
nates; combined elasticities of either sign are consistent
with theory. Again, except for several results deduced
from Feldstein, all combined elasticities are small in magnitude. The vast majority fall between -0.1 and +0.1;
virtually all (except for Feldstein) fall between -0.2 and
+0.2.
     Recall that the range of -0.2 to +0.2 is deduced from
studies that concentrate primarily on the northeastern and
midwestern states, where private education is of relatively greater significance than elsewhere. If a 1 percent
change in private enrollment in these states induces expenditure changes of this magnitude, a 1 percent change
elsewhere is likely to induce even smaller changes; a 1
percent increase in private enrollments that are already
relatively large must have a larger impact on the political process than a 1 percent increase in private enrollments that are of inconsequential magnitude. Therefore,
the range of -0.2 to +0.2 for the combined elasticity
should represent the outer limits of the effects on public
expenditure that are likely to occur.

TAX CREDIT AND PUBLIC EXPENDITURE
     The tax credit's effect on expenditure may be en-
visioned as occurring in two separate stages: (1) the
credit induces an increase in private enrollment accompanied by a commensurate decrease in public enrollment;
(2) the increased private enrollment causes the political
process to adjust public per pupil expenditures. (No effort is made here to deal with possible secondary effects,
such as an additional exodus from the public sector induced by the possible reduction of expenditures.)
     In order to estimate the enrollment effect of a tui-
tion tax credit similar to those proposed, refer to chapter 3 where private enrollment changes were projected as
part of the exercise of estimating the revenues lost because of a tax credit. The first column of Table 5.3 re-
peats the estimated total (elementary plus secondary) enrollment increases calculated in chapter 3 under a variety
of assumptions. All enrollment increases assume a tax
credit of 50 percent to a maximum of $500. The first two
rows show the effects of this hypothetical credit in the
benchmark year of 1978; the last two, for 1985. The two
1978 estimates are similar, whether the narrow or broad

Table 5.3. Effects of 50% Credit on Private Enrollment and Public Expenditure

Assumptions	Estimated % Change of Private Enrollment	% Change of Public per Pupil Expenditure	
		Combined Elasticity −0.2	Combined Elasticity +0.2
Nominal definition of tuition, 1978[a]	12.2	−2.4	+2.4
Broad definition of tuition, 1978[b]	15.1	−3.0	+3.0
Nominal definition of tuition, 1985[c]	9.3	−1.9	+1.9
Nominal definition of tuition, with 25% state credits, 1985[d]	16.1	−3.2	+3.2

[a]Table 3.1, B.
[b]Table 3.1, C.
[c]Table 3.4, B.
[d]Table 3.4, C.

definition of tuition is used: enrollment increases 12 or 15 percent.[10] The largest enrollment increase of 16 percent (row 4) occurs only in conjunction with the assumption of state tuition tax credits being introduced in the aftermath of a federal credit.

The second and third columns show the impact on per pupil expenditure of each enrollment change under the assumptions of −0.2 and +0.2 elasticities, respectively, of per pupil expenditure with respect to private enrollment. The largest range of expenditure changes occurs in row 4, with per pupil changes between −3.2 and +3.2 percent assuming 25 percent state tax credits. The second-largest projected impact on per pupil expenditures is in the range −3.0 to +3.0 percent; assuming the broad definition of tuition. The smallest projected range is −1.9 to +1.9, where estimated inflation in 1985 tuition rates reduces enrollment impact of a capped credit and keeps the overall impact on public expenditures low.[11]

CONCLUSION

The finding that the negative impact of a credit is likely to be at most −3.2 percent and that the impact may instead be positive makes it difficult to conclude on the basis of existing evidence, that a tuition tax credit of the type studied here represents a great threat to per pupil expenditures in the public sector. The variability of the elasticity estimates and their small magnitudes suggest that the potential impact of a credit on support for public expenditures should not be a major consideration in assessing the desirability of a tax credit.

NOTES

    1. The precise amount of taxes an individual tax-
payer would owe depends also on the total tax base of the
community and the taxpayer's share of the tax base.
    2. This is a standard result. To the left of X*,
additional increments to public-school expenditures would
bring the taxpayer more utility than is lost by giving up
the required amount of private consumption, and vice versa.
    3. There is an alternate way to obtain this result.
Consider that as the number of pupils is reduced, higher
levels of per pupil expenditures are required to raise education taxes enough to reduce a taxpayer's after-tax income to zero. This may be envisioned as a movement of the
right vertical axis to the right as enrollment declines.
Since the marginal utility of private consumption curve
maintains its position relative to the right axis, any
given level of per pupil expenditure will now be associated with a lower marginal utility of private goods. Note
that the same logic dictates that any reduction in the individual taxpayer's share of the total public tax bill
would have the same effect as a reduction in the number of
pupils.
    4. Of course, if there is universal education and
if the general public cannot readily distinguish between
public- and private-school pupils, then most citizens probably would not perceive the loss of external benefits flow-
ing from a reduction of public-school pupils.
    5. The displaced consumption must have been of less
utility than private schooling, or it would not have been
displaced. The credit has induced a family to spend its
after-tax income differently--more private education,
fewer other goods. This voluntary change in spending
patterns occurs only when it is thereby possible to obtain
higher utility from marginal expenditures.
    6. This is because the tuition payments are likely
to be far larger than any tax reductions caused by the
overall reduction of public enrollments.
    7. Holding the tax base per pupil constant while
enrollment declines is equivalent to requiring the taxpayer
to pay the same dollar amount of taxes to sustain any given
per pupil expenditure despite the declining enrollment.
This is not a real possibility, rather a conceptual exper-
iment that could only be carried out with multiple regression analysis; it would be possible only if a proportion-

ate amount of the property tax base were being removed as
enrollment declined so that the remaining taxpayers continued to pay as much as before.

8. Since any change in public enrollment creates a
known change in tax base per pupil, one can easily calculate the indirect effect on per pupil expenditures. For
example, suppose p_2 is converted into elasticity form and
indicates that a 1 percent increase in tax base per pupil
increases per pupil expenditures 0.2 percent. We know how
much a given increase in public enrollment changes tax base
per pupil (all else being equal): for example, doubling
enrollment halves the tax base per pupil. Suppose a tax
credit decreased public enrollment by 25 percent; this implies a 33 percent increase of tax base per pupil. So the
indirect effect of the 25 percent decrease of public enrollment would be $(33)(0.2) = 6.6$ percent.

9. The major assumption underlying the conversion
of results stated in terms of public enrollments into results in terms of private enrollments is that for any
given community, private enrollment displaces public enrollment on a one-for-one basis.

10. Note that if private enrollment is initially 0.1
of public enrollment, a 15 percent increase in private enrollment would imply only a 1.5 percent decrease in public
enrollment.

11. Were the largest combined elasticities deduced
from the Feldstein study accepted, the range of effects
would be far larger. At their extremes, these estimated
elasticities imply a reduction of public expenditures of
as much as 24 percent or an increase of as much as 19 percent.

REFERENCES: TABLES 5.1, 5.2

Cohn, E. *Economics of State Aid to Education* (Lexington,
        Mass.: Heath, 1974).
Davis, O. In *Public Economy of Urban Communities,* ed.
        J. Margolis (Washington, D. C.: Resources for the
        Future, 1965).
Denzau, A. "An Empirical Survey of Studies of Public
        School Spending," *National Tax Journal* (June 1975).
Feldstein, M. "Wealth Neutrality and Local Choice in
        Public Education," *American Economic Review* (March
        1975).

Frey, D. In *Restoring Confidence in Public Education:
     Conference Research Papers* (Washington, D. C.:
     National Urban Coalition, 1979).

Grubb, N., and J. Osman. "The Causes of School Finance
     Inequalities: Serrano and the Case of California,"
     Public Finance Quarterly (July, 1977).

Gustman, A., and G. Pidot. "Interactions between Education-
     al Spending and Student Enrollment," *Journal of Human
     Resources* (Winter, 1973).

Ladd, H. "Local Education Expenditures, Fiscal Capacity
     and the Composition of the Property Tax Base,"
     National Tax Journal (June, 1975).

Lovell, M. "Spending for Education: The Exercise of
     Public Choice," *Review of Economics and Statistics*
     (November, 1978).

Miner, J. *Social and Economic Factors in Spending for
     Public Education* (Syracuse, N. Y.: Syracuse Univ.
     Press, 1963)

CHAPTER 6

Tax Credit Benefits

The empirical work of chapter 2 is particularly well suited to the kinds of analyses done in chapters 3-5; therefore, the study focuses on the potential public costs imposed by a tuition tax credit of the type generally proposed. To a more limited extent, we may utilize the same analytical framework to assess the degree to which a tuition tax credit would produce benefits for the public.

TARGET EFFICIENCY

Target efficiency has been proposed as a criterion for judging the effectiveness of public programs in attaining stated objectives.[1] A program is defined here as x percent target efficient if x percent of the total dollars spent actually are received by the intended beneficiaries or represent the value of an intended output. Estimates of the total cost of a 50 percent ($500 maximum) tuition tax credit have already been presented (chapter 3). What proportions of this cost might contribute directly to the stated objectives of the tuition tax credit? For example, if the stated goal is to provide tax relief for the middle class, what proportion of the total cost of the credit would actually go to middle-class taxpayers? The objectives of a tuition tax credit have been stated in proposed bills, in testimony before committees of Congress, and in numerous pamphlets and articles. When overlapping objectives are consolidated, at least three distinct objectives can be observed:

1. The enhancement of private choice in matters of education.

2. Tax relief in general, or specifically for the middle class.

3. The equalizing of educational opportunity.

Although these are stated somewhat abstractly it may be possible to produce operational definitions of each of these objectives.

Enhancement of Private Choice

In order to estimate the efficiency of the tax credit in enhancing private choice, we must first define whose choice has been enhanced. The only group for whom it is certain that choice has been enhanced is the group that changes its objective behavior because of the enactment of the tax credit. That is, only switchers (families who switch their children from public to private schools in response to the credit) have clearly indicated that their choice has been enhanced. If a tax credit fails to change a family's choice of schools, there is no objective basis for claiming that the family's choice has been enhanced; families that continue to use public schools despite the credit's enactment and families that already used private schools before the credit have not had their choice enhanced in any observable way. In view of this, the target efficiency of the credit in enhancing private choice will be defined as the proportion of the total cost of the credit that actually is received by families whose choice of schools is observably affected (i.e., switchers).

The target efficiency of the credit in enhancing choice is shown in Table 6.1. The table puts results implicit in chapter 3 into usable form. The major finding is that for a hypothetical credit of 50 percent ($500 maximum) in 1978, only about 12 or 13 percent of the total lost revenues actually would have gone to switchers; moving the frame of reference to a hypothetical 1985 credit (Table

Table 6.1. Target Efficiency of Hypothetical 50% Credit in Enhancing Choice: 1978

Basis of Calculations	Total New Private Enrollment[a] (000)	Total Credit Benefits to New Enrollees[b] ($000)	Total Cost of Credit[c] ($000)	Efficiency Ratio Col.2/Col.3
Nominal tuition	549	197,207	1,671,222	.12
Broad tuition	675	285,988	2,220,586	.13

Source: First row derived from Table 3.1, B; second row derived from Table 3.1, C.

[a]Total enrollments (Table 3.1, B or C) - total precredit enrollments (A).
[b]Average credits for elementary and for secondary students (Table 3.1) x increment in enrollments, respectively, and summed.
[c]Total lost revenues, Table 3.1, B, C.

3.4) would not have improved the efficiency ratio. Another way to state the result is that of every $8 in lost tax revenues, only $1 would be paid to someone whose education-al choice was actually affected by the credit. The other $7 goes to those whose behavior is unaffected and who, in essence, receive the credit as a windfall gain (neglecting the portion captured by the schools through higher tuition fees).[2]

Can the credit's efficiency with respect to choice enhancement be improved? So long as the number of students in private schools prior to enactment of the credit is large relative to the number likely to be switchers, the credit's efficiency in this respect must be small. Only if the demand and supply elasticities were other than we have estimated them could this be different. Further, there is no apparent way to grant credits equitably to switchers while denying credits to those already in pri-vate schools, which would be another method for increas-ing the target efficiency.

Middle Class Tax Relief

The benchmark study for analysis of the costs of a tuition tax credit in chapter 3 provides a significant amount of detail on the beneficiaries of a tuition tax credit. According to the study, a hypothetical 50 percent credit in 1978 would have directed 48 percent of elemen-tary – level benefits to the middle class and 39 percent of secondary-level benefits to the middle class.[3] Although this study ignores the enrollment response to a tax credit, it is not likely that it would significantly change the results.

The target efficiency of the credit could be im-proved significantly if middle-class tax relief were the major goal. There is ample precedent for limiting tax benefits to families whose incomes fall within some bounds. This would have the potential of improving target effi-ciency dramatically.[4]

Relief from Education Taxes

E. G. West has argued that a tuition tax credit, while costly to the federal government, has the potential for reducing education taxes at the local level.[5] The es-sence of the argument is that for every child induced by the credit to switch to the private sector, local taxpay-ers save on expenditures for public education. West argues further that it is possible for the savings on local education to outweigh the cost in lost federal revenues because the average expenditure on public education is larger than the tax credit is likely to be.[6] The West argument implies that essentially the same taxpayers would gain at the local level what is lost at the federal; if this were not so, the West mechanism would raise problems of redistribution of the tax burden, which he does not address.

In this analysis, every child induced to switch to the private sector by a credit represents a net gain to taxpayers (who pay both federal and local taxes). For example, a maximum federal credit of $500 would relieve the local government of average public-school expenditures of as much as $1700, a net gain of $1200.[7] The problem, of course, is that children previously enrolled in private schools are also eligible for the credit; each of them also costs $500 in lost federal revenue with no offsetting reduction in local expenses. (This is not to say that private-school attendance by these children does not in some way relieve the public of education expenses; rather, that a credit paid to these children fails to provide any new local relief.) Thus, in the West scheme, the public savings obtained from the children who are induced by the credit to switch to the private sector is offset by the credit payments made to students already in the private sector, who in essence receive a windfall gain. The crucial question becomes whether enough students would be induced to switch to make the credit produce an overall tax saving for the public.

It is possible to assess the efficiency of the tax credit in producing the kind of tax savings defined by West. Table 6.2 gathers several pertinent results from chapter 3; the only new information included is West's estimate for average public, per pupil expenditures. We see that a hypothetical 50 percent credit in 1978 would have induced an enrollment switch of some 549,000 pupils,

Table 6.2. Savings on Public Education Expenditures as a Result of Hypothetical 50% Credit: 1978

Estimated Postcredit Private Enrollment (000)	Estimated Increase in Private Enrollment (000)	Estimated Local Savings on Public Schools[a] ($000)	Total Lost Federal Revenue ($000)	Local Savings ÷ Federal Revenue Lost
5026	549	953,064	1,671,222	0.57

Source: Based on Table 3.1, B.
[a]Col. 2 x public per pupil expenditure of $1736.

which according to West's figure would have saved local
taxpayers $953,064,000 on public education. Yet, the
total cost of the credit is higher still, $1.67 billion.
Thus, the credit produces local tax relief of only $0.57
for every dollar of lost revenue to the federal government.
        The calculations in Table 6.2 give the maximum mag-
nitude of West-type tax savings at the local level, for
they assume that public expenditures would be reduced by
the full average per pupil expenditure for every student
that switches into private schools. However, evidence
shows that public school districts tend in the short run
to reduce expenditures less than the proportion of enrollment changes; that is, the public's savings are less than
average per pupil expenditures.[8]

Equality of Educational Opportunity
        The objective of "equality of educational opportun-
ity" is open to interpretation. Nothing in the proposed
legislation, for example, suggests that the attainment of
equality would require reducing high educational opportunities for anyone. Presumably the object of the tax credit
is to increase the opportunities for children with below
average opportunity. Since all the tuition tax credit
does specifically is to provide monetary resources, opportunity logically may be interpreted as being advanced
through receiving or benefiting from funds. Thus, no direct gains from the tax credit would be available to public-sector pupils.[9] Two clearly identifiable ways that
low-opportunity students may find their opportunities increased are:

        1. The credit will permit some to switch from
public schools to private schools that are presumably
better from the students' perspective.
        2. Students already in private schools may receive
the benefit of increased per pupil expenditures as the
credit permits private schools to charge more.

        Table 6.3 summarizes the efficiency of the tax cred-
it (based on nominal tuition) in terms of the proportion
of dollars channeled into these two uses. It is assumed
that low-opportunity and low-income are synonymous terms.
We see that only 0.9 of 1 percent of credit funds are directed to new, low-income private-school users; and only
2.9 percent of the funds represent incremental spending

Table 6.3.   Target Efficiency of 50% Tax Credit in Enhancing
      Equality of Opportunity: 1978

Enrollment (000)	Benefits Received ($000)	Credit Benefits[a] ($000)	Efficiency Ratio (2)/(3)
A. New, low-income private school users			
49	14,547	1,671,222	.009
B. Incremental expenditures on precredit, low-income private students			
412	48,116[b]	1,671,222	.029
C. Incremental expenditure on all precredit private students			
4477	677,482[c]	1,671,222	.41

Source: Parts A and B from Tables 3.3, Table 3.1; C from Table 3.1,
A, B.
   [a]Based on cost estimate of Table 3.1, B.
   [b]Increment is tuition in Table 3.3, B - tuition in Table 3.3, A.
Increments are multiplied by respective enrollments and summed.
   [c]Increment is tuition in Table 3.1, B - tuition in A. Increments
are multiplied by respective enrollments and summed.

on all low-income private-school users. Even together,
the target efficiency is less than 4 percent.
      One interpretation of "equalizing educational oppor-
tunity" may result in a higher efficiency ratio. Average
per pupil spending in the private sector is substantially
less than that in the public; in that sense almost all
private-school students do not have equal opportunity.
Therefore, any incremental private-school expenditures
that can be attributed to the credit may be viewed as per-
forming the equalizing role. Suppose that all induced increases in the tuition charged by private schools ulti-
mately benefit the enrolled students and that this represents equalization relative to the public sector; under
this interpretation of equalizing opportunity, target efficiency reaches 41 percent (part C).

Conclusions on Target Efficiency

      As a device for enhancing educational choice, the
tax credit is target inefficient, delivering only about
one dollar of every eight spent to those whose choice has
demonstrably been enhanced by the credit. As a device for
providing tax relief, the tax credit has a target efficiency of somewhat less than 50 percent if middle-class
relief is the goal and somewhat more than 50 percent if
West-type tax relief is the goal. Finally, as a device
for equalizing educational opportunity, the results are
mixed. If the definition of educational opportunity focuses on low-income students, the tax credit is target inefficient. If the definition focuses on the spending differential between the total public and total private sectors, then the efficiency of the credit is as high as 40
or 41 percent.

TAX CREDIT AND RESTRICTIVE ZONING PRACTICES
     It has been argued that in urban areas with seg-
mented political jurisdictions, as are often found in the
metropolitan Northeast, citizens sort themselves into in-
ternally homogeneous communities, each of which provides
the mix of public services and tax rates most preferred
by the group of citizens living there.[10] This multijuris-
dictional metropolitan area produces problems as well as
benefits. Local property taxes pay for the services provided, and families pay roughly in proportion to the value
of the housing they consume. This creates an obvious incentive for families that consume only a small amount of
housing (e.g., apartment dwellers) to move into jurisdictions offering a high level of services, since they could
enjoy the services while paying considerably less than the
average amount of tax.
     The response to this has been that the residents of
a community employ zoning restrictions on certain types of
housing or lot sizes to guarantee that everyone in the community must consume enough housing to pay a fair share of
taxes. The negative aspect of this is that low-income,
often minority, families are excluded from such communities.
     Because schooling is one of the main services pro-
vided locally, a link exists between the level of public
education provided in a community and restrictive zoning.
Two distinct ways exist for breaking this link. One way
is to finance public education from nonlocal sources, such
as state aid, removing the link between the local level of
expenditure on education and the local level of taxes;
there would be no longer an incentive to engage in exclu-
sionary zoning.[11] The second way to break the link is to
increase the probability that low-income residents of a
community do not choose to utilize the public schools,
thus imposing no cost to the community. It then does not
matter that they may choose to live within the community.
     The tax credit is unlikely to serve as a method of
shifting public education funding to higher levels of government. While it is possible that a broadly worded tuition tax credit bill might allow public schools to charge
tuition so as to take advantage of the federal tax credit,
the cost of this to the federal government would be substantial; public school enrollment is so much larger than
private school enrollment that the cost would jump dramatically. Congress is very unlikely to use language that

would permit public schools to shift any substantial portion of their costs to the federal government.

The tuition tax credit would increase the incidence of nonpublic enrollment among all income groups, including lower income groups. However, the incidence of private enrollment is unlikely to jump substantially. A community would continue to view any potential lower income residents as having approximately the same probability of entering the public schools after the tax credit as before.

These considerations make it unlikely that the tuition tax credit would contribute substantially to reducing the practice of restrictive zoning.

NOTES

1. *Federal Aid to Postsecondary Students: Tax Allowances and Alternative Subsidies* (Washington, D. C.: Congressional Budget Office, 1978).

2. The low target efficiency of the tuition tax credit with respect to private choice enhancement is unlikely to deter those who favor the credit for philosophical reasons (e.g., laissez-faire notions of pure consumer sovereignty). The efficiency of the instrument is of only secondary concern.

Consumer sovereignty as a norm for judging public programs, however, has two problems. The first is that no government can use consumer choice alone as a criterion for judging programs. Governments are inevitably involved with the content of choices, not the mere act of private choice. The second problem is philosophical. The economic philosophy of consumer sovereignty ignores how the values are formed that dictate how choice will be exercised. If these values are not fixed, but are learned and shaped over time, then consumers may come eventually to prefer those things that they might not have chosen originally. In education, parents who might be unhappy with the prospect of public education might eventually come to prefer public schools after experience with them. (Gallup surveys consistently show that parents of public school students rate the public schools more favorably than parents of non-public pupils.)

3. Martha J. Jacobs, "Tuition Tax Credits for Elementary and Secondary Education: Some Evidence," *J. Ed.*

Finance 5: Table 4. Middle class is here defined in terms
of incomes of families in the $10,000 to $25,000 per year
range in 1978 when the median family income was about
$17,000. Although a family with an income of, say,
$40,000 in 1978 may have been middle class in the sense of
attitudes or habits, such an income was more than twice
the median and placed that family in the top several percent by income.

4. The April 1982 proposal of the Reagan administration did involve phasing out tax credit benefits for families with incomes above $50,000. The 1983 proposal in-
volves a phaseout above $40,000.

5. E. G. West, *The Economics of Education Tax
Credits* (Washington, D. C.: Heritage Foundation, 1981),
28–29.

6. The average credit should be less than the average public expenditure per pupil for two reasons. First,
private per pupil expenditures are on the average less
than public per pupil expenditures. Second, most major
tuition tax credit proposals envisage a less than 100 percent reimbursement.

7. Note that this discussion does not involve the
kinds of effects that were the subject of chapter 5.

8. Donald Frey, "The Impact of School Finance Re-
form on Indicators of Expenditure Inequality," *Econ. Ed.
Rev.* 1(1981): 353.

9. Some have suggested that public-school pupils
would benefit indirectly as competition from private
schools made the public systems more responsive. Or, in
line with the reasoning of chapter 5, the political process
might produce an increase in per pupil expenditures in the
public schools as public enrollment declined. This would
presumably benefit low-opportunity students in public
schools. These possibilities are both clearly speculative.

10. J. Vernon Henderson, *Economic Theory and the
Cities* (New York: Academic Press, 1977), 213–216.

11. Of course, having the state take over the financing of local education may just reintroduce the problem in
a new form. If state education is to be equitable, it
would have to pay each community the same amount per pupil
(with perhaps some adjustments for differences in costs).
Any community wishing to spend more than the state average
would have to levy local taxes to produce a local supple-
ment, thus reintroducing the problem in a modified fashion.

CHAPTER 7

Beyond Quantitative Analysis

SUMMARY
     Several results have emerged from the study of the
tuition tax credit. The private sector in education can
be analyzed by economic techniques commonly used to study
other kinds of markets, thus making available powerful
quantitative tools to assess the impact of a tuition tax
credit. The magnitude of the federal revenue loss likely
to be caused by a tuition tax credit is estimated and is
found to be substantially larger than typically estimated
in government projections. This loss is greater yet if
state governments also offer tuition tax credits, thereby
increasing further private enrollments and those eligible
to claim the federal credit. If the practice of parents
making "donations" in lieu of tuition payments to private
schools is widespread, a tax credit would produce a powerful incentive to absorb donations into a new, larger tuition payment against which the credit would be claimed.
Again, this would add to the federal revenue loss in a way
apparently not contemplated by government officials. Also,
inflation would tend to reduce the federal revenue loss associated with a capped tuition tax credit; this reduction
would be in terms of both money and real purchasing power.
The obvious interpretation is that inflation would produce
strong political pressure to maintain the value of the tax
credit by removing or raising any limit on credit benefits.
     Enrollment switching between public and private
schools would be a major consequence of a tuition subsidy
such as the tax credit. Under a wide range of conditions,
the proportion of minority students in urban public school
systems would be increased by a tuition tax credit; however,
it appears that this increase would be relatively small. A

statistical correlation between increased minority concentration and increased segregation in public school districts exists; thus a tuition tax credit might simultaneously increase minority concentration and segregation. If public schools had minority-student proportions as low as
those found in the private sector, then segregation would
be as low in the public sector as some have claimed it to
be in the private.

A theory of voter behavior is developed and is found
to be incapable of unambiguously projecting the way a tuition tax credit might influence voter support for public-
school expenditure levels. A survey of several empirical
studies of per pupil expenditure levels in communities with
varying rates of private enrollment also produced ambiguous
results: increased private enrollment sometimes seems correlated with slight reductions and sometimes with slight
increases of public, per pupil expenditures. The theoretical and empirical evidence now available does not appear
to support concern that the tuition tax credit, by increasing private enrollment rates, would seriously undermine
voter support for public schools.

Several categories of benefits claimed for tuition
tax credits are examined. The major finding is that no
single objective of the tax credit can be obtained with
fiscal efficiency. In general, several dollars of federal
revenue loss would be generated for each dollar reaching a
specific group of intended beneficiaries.

BEYOND THE FRAMEWORK
These results were produced within the confines of a
fairly rigid framework of economic analysis. To be sure,
the approach has its merits. The tax credit is certainly
an economic device, so an economic approach seems logical;
further, the approach is explicit about its view of the
way things work--what is essential to an understanding of
the problem and what may be ignored. The use of explicit,
mathematical formulas to define key relationships means
that shaky conclusions are easily seen; if slight changes
in key variables or parameters or slight respecifications
of the formulas vastly change the results, then a highly
contingent nature of the results is obvious.

The weakness of this kind of approach is that it is
static--using the before-and-after snapshot method. The
method amounts to extracting key statistical relationships
from the private-education market and subjecting them to

various manipulations to see how the market would react to
a tax credit. In short, the private-education market that
has existed in the recent past--as summed up in equations--
is forced to react to a tax credit according to standard
economic rules. Then the two states of the market are
compared to measure the impact of the credit.

The private-education market of the near future probably will resemble that of the recent past, so this method
has some merit; yet, what if the private sector in education were on the verge of major changes? This method could
not anticipate the changes and the results might therefore
be invalidated. Thus it is worth assessing the probability
that either of two potential changes in private education
may occur and what their occurrence would mean. One change
that could potentially transform private education would
occur as the result of a massive collapse of public confidence in public education. The second change would occur
as a consequence of a major shift of private enrollment
from North to South.

Failure of Confidence in Public Education?

Throughout this study the educational environment into which a tuition tax credit would be introduced is assumed to be what has existed in the recent past. Suppose,
however, that public confidence in public education were
to decline dramatically in the near future. This might
cause a large, unexpected increase in private enrollment,
resulting in a loss of federal revenues far in excess of
our estimations. Projections of school segregation might
also change.

The likelihood of this happening may be judged by
means of the Gallup surveys of public opinion about education, which have been conducted since 1968. Since 1974 the
annual poll has asked respondents to rate public schools on
a scale from A to F, the way students are usually graded.
In 1974 the top two categories were chosen by 48 percent of
the respondents, in 1977 by only 37 percent, a level that
roughly has held since then.[1] At the same time the proportion assigning the schools a failing or poor grade has
risen consistently.

So a dramatic collapse of public confidence in public
education already has occurred. Significantly, the private
schools' enrollments did not benefit. Enrollment data published by the Current Population Survey (CPS) and the National Center for Education Statistics (NCES), while not
identical, permit the conclusion that private schools

failed to capitalize on the large drop of confidence in the
public schools. The CPS shows the private share of all enrollment declining from 10.6 (1970) to 9.3 percent (1974),
then rising to 10.2 percent (1978) before dropping again
to 9.8 percent the next year.[2] The NCES figures (Table
1.2) show a slight rise in share from 10.1 (1970-1971) to
10.7 percent (1978-1979). Either way, private enrollment
did not gain dramatically in response to the middecade decline of confidence in the public schools.

   Why this failure? Perhaps the collapse of confidence
was not so great among those in a position to make enrollment decisions as among the public in general. The Gallup
survey shows that parents of children actually attending
public schools rate those schools more positively than do
others.[3] Furthermore, those least satisfied are not the
parents of private-school children but nonparents, who are
in no position to influence enrollment patterns and who
have the least first-hand information about public schools.
This is one reason the decline of confidence in public education did not cause a large enrollment shift.

   Another possibility is that confidence in private
education was undergoing a decline at the same time. If
this were true, then private schooling would gain no advantage over public schooling in public opinion, there
would be no reason to expect private enrollment to increase
relative to total enrollment. Such a decline of confidence
in private schooling cannot be documented because the Gallup poll does not ask such a question; however, it cannot
be ruled out. If the attraction of Roman Catholic schools,
for example, has traditionally been their religious atmo-
sphere, the tendency of the last decade or more for these
schools to rely more on lay teachers as the religious orders have declined in numbers may have produced a lessen-
ing of confidence among these schools' usual clientele.[4]

   Although the causes are the subject of ongoing spec-
ulation, a large decline in public confidence in the public schools during the mid-1970s did fail to produce a
substantial switching of enrollment to the private sector.
Therefore, it seems exceedingly unlikely that in the near
future any further decline of confidence in the public
schools would trigger an exodus, thus upsetting the conclusions of the study. Even if a further decline in confidence were assumed, one would have to make the additional assumption that the private sector would gain from it--
something it failed to do previously.

The largest decline of confidence occurred between 1974 and 1977; the public sector has held its own since then. This stabilization suggests that another decline of confidence is not likely. Those citizens most susceptible to losing confidence in public education undoubtedly did so during the mid-1970s, and a further decline of confidence would require shaking the views of those less susceptible.

Regional Composition of Enrollment

The CPS documents two changes in the composition of private enrollments culminating during the 1970s: a decline of Roman Catholic enrollment from about 85 percent to about 67 percent of all private enrollment, and the increase of the relative proportion of private enrollment in the South and West at the expense of the Northeast and North Central regions.[5] These changes are related because Roman Catholic schools are most heavily concentrated in the North and North Central regions. The South--and to a much lesser degree the West--gained not only in proportion, but in absolute numbers.[6] The overall effect was that private enrollment moved South, although as a group private schools retained a fairly static share of total U.S. enrollment.

In this section the trend is assumed to continue strongly; and the ways that such a trend would force modifications of earlier conclusions are considered. Specifically, the discussions in this section assume that enrollment in southern private schools will increase at the expense of northern private schools, with the overall proportion of private enrollment for the nation remaining roughly constant. This would produce a private sector different from the one upon which projections in earlier chapters are based, and the earlier conclusions will necessarily be modified.

It is necessary to warn, however, that such an exaggerated trend in the future seems unlikely. It seems highly probable that much of the gain of private enrollment in the South in the 1970s was due to the transition from segregated schools to integrated schools. This transition is now over and is not apt to generate further gains in private enrollments in the South. Whether the growth of religious fundamentalist schools could generate such a large enrollment shift is considered later, but it also seems unlikely.

If a tuition tax credit were implemented at a time
when private enrollment was much more concentrated in the
South than in the recent past, the cost to the federal
government would be larger than projected in this study
because the private tuition is higher in the South than
elsewhere.[7] The obvious effect of concentrating private
enrollment in the South is that more students would be
eligible for larger credits.

Without engaging in a full-fledged technical study,
only the roughest estimates of the additional federal revenue loss may be given. Yet, even an exceptionally simple
analysis may provide some sense of the extra revenue loss
associated with shifting one million private students from
the Northeast and North Central to the South. If we assume zero demand elasticity--not because it is correct but
because it is simple--and also assume that such an enrollment shift would not affect prevailing tuition rates in
North and South--another unlikely but simplifying assump-
tion--we discover that federal revenue losses would be
about $175 million per year larger than previously esti-
mated.[8] Because this figure is based on two simplifying
assumptions that tend to produce underestimates of revenue
loss, it seems reasonable that an enrollment switch of one
million to the South--keeping overall private enrollment
constant--would cost the federal government perhaps $200
million a year more than projected earlier. Naturally,
any enrollment shift of less than a million students would
produce proportionately smaller extra revenue losses.

Although it seems unlikely that desegregation would
produce large future gains of private enrollment in the
South, it is likely that if such gains did occur--for whatever reason--the majority of students switching to private
schools would be white. The inevitable result is that
minority proportions in the public schools of the South
would increase; enacting a tuition tax credit would further exaggerate the pattern. Of course, if private enrollment gained in the South while declining in the North,
one might expect the opposite, compensating effect in the
North; some reduction of minority proportions in the public
schools in the North.

Offsetting effects on racial composition in the public schools of the South and North would occur, however
only if school districts in the different regions were or-
ganized similarly. In the South, a central-city area and
its surrounding suburbs are often included in a single
school district, while in the North the central city usual-

ly is a separate district surrounded by several independent suburban districts.[9] Thus, white students in the South would typically move from a unified urban-suburban district (where their presence would contribute to integration) to private schools; in the North, any white students gained by public schools would probably reinforce the predominantly white suburban school systems and contribute little to integration of the central district. This asymmetry between North and South implies that any integration gain in the North would be smaller than the loss that an exodus to private schools would produce in the South. This organization of urban southern school districts is an important reason why legal remedies such as busing have generally worked to produce integration better there than elsewhere.[10] This means that the hypothesized increase of private enrollments in the South would reduce enrollments in the public systems contributing most to the nation's record on integration. Conversely, the loss of private enrollment assumed for the North would increase enrollments in public systems contributing the least of the nation's progress.

This kind of discussion forces one to return to the fundamental issue of whether a massive shift of enrollment of the private sector to the South is plausible. As previously mentioned, if desegregation lay in the future instead of the past, it might provide grounds for speculating that private enrollment in the South would grow. Another possible driving force for private-school expansion would be the growth of fundamentalist Protestant schools. Is fundamentalism capable of producing a massive growth of private schooling in the South or are its prospects limited?

The means by which fundamentalist schools differentiated themselves from public schools probably impose limits to their potential expansion. Because they must appeal to a potential clientele that is part of the socioeconomic majority, they cannot rely on socioeconomic distinctiveness. Instead, fundamentalist schools tend to base their appeal on ideological grounds, which require their curriculum to be strongly differentiated from that of public schools. The direction that this differentiation takes is a rejection of significant segments of modern learning, for example the substitution of "creation science" for modern biology.

Differentiating the curriculum this way increases the appeal of fundamentalist schools to some, but it also inevitably makes such schools unacceptable to large numbers of parents. By adopting a confrontational posture toward modern learning--most acute in the issue of evolution but

apparent throughout--such schools guarantee that they will
fail to appeal to all except those who already share a
highly particular view of reality. In a nation where
regional differences tend to blur and where society is in-
creasingly pluralistic, this strategy of sharp curriculum
differentiation limits the appeal of such schools.

The conclusion casts doubt on the proposition that a
major enrollment switch awaits in the near future. The
projections of the earlier chapters seem secure.

POLITICS AND THE TUITION TAX CREDIT

Government aid to private education has had more success in legislatures than among voters. The National Education Association lists eleven referendums between 1967
and 1981 regarding some form of state aid to private education, all of which lost by substantial margins.[11] In 1982
two additional private-school aid referendums lost with
negative votes of more than 60 percent.[12] Of most significance was the loss by a margin of nine to one of a tuition
tax credit measure in Washington, D. C., in 1981. While
the margin of defeat may have reflected (in part) the exceptionally generous benefits built into the proposal, it
is still a remarkable defeat, for 1981 may have been the
high-water mark of the recent conservative swing in American politics. In fact, the perception that the District
of Columbia proposal was part of a larger conservative
agenda for education may have contributed to the margin
of defeat.

Despite this poor record with voters, aid for private
schools, including tax subsidies of various sorts, has been
more successful in legislatures. (Most of these bills have
been invalidated in the courts. See chapter 1.) Obviously,
intense lobbying by those with much to gain is able to produce results that the electorate generally does not seem
to desire, but this may not be the only reason for the different results. In a referendum before the voters, a
single issue must stand or fall on its own merits; in the
legislature, on the contrary, an issue like the tuition tax
credit may become linked to some other issue. For example,
legislators may vote for tuition tax credits to show they
are for middle-class tax relief even if they would prefer
some other vehicle to demonstrate their loyalties.

Over the years the tuition tax credit has been considered a nonpartisan or at least a bipartisan issue. How-

ever, during 1981 and 1982 the concept has begun to bear
the burden of a partisan association. By introducing its
tax credit plan in the broader context of plans to discon-
tinue the U.S. Department of Education, to reduce federal
aid to public schools, and to prevent the IRS from denying
tax exemption to discriminatory schools, the Reagan administration has essentially identified the tuition tax credit
with its own, exceptionally conservative program. Such an
identification is not a burden that the tuition tax credit
has borne in the past, although philosophical support for
state aid of private schools has come primarily from con-
servatives.

Continuing large federal deficits, projected for most
of the remainder of this decade, must also be viewed as a
hindrance to possible passage of a tuition tax credit. In
view of large projected deficits, the Reagan administration
in the fall of 1982 scaled down its April 1982 tax-credit
proposal. A smaller proposal was resubmitted in 1983 (see
chapter 3) after the 1982 proposal failed. Despite the
large deficits, the administration may feel that it should
strive to have tuition tax credits accepted in principle
so that increases could be legislated at a later date as a
matter of course.

A great political unknown is whether a tuition tax
credit for private elementary and secondary education can
be enacted without the passage of a tax credit for higher
education. Originally the tuition tax credit was proposed
exclusively for higher education; it is highly ironic that
at present it is proposed solely for elementary and secondary schools. The reason the Reagan administration omitted
higher education is obvious: the projected addition to
the federal deficit it would involve--even allowing for the
tendency of government analysts to understate revenue loss--
would be so large as to spell defeat of such a proposal.
However, proponents of the elementary and secondary credit
might be unable to keep the colleges and universities out
of the picture. The higher education lobby is almost certainly stronger than the private-school lobby. If a tax
credit for private schools would be so costly as to require cost savings elsewhere in the federal education budget, higher education might climb aboard a tax-credit bill
as a defensive measure. Given the federal deficit, this
would surely doom the proposal.

Since 1981 the prospects for a tuition tax credit
have dimmed. The packaging of the credit with other edu-

cation proposals that are identified with the extreme political right has hurt the plan as have rising federal deficits and omitting higher education. The 1983 decision of
the Supreme Court that a Minnesota tax deduction for education expenses was constitutional may have been a Pyrrhic
victory for the cause of a federal tuition tax credit, because constitutionality is now predicated on a credit's
being available for almost any education expenditure--not
just private-school tuition. (This requirement makes
church-affiliated, private schools only incidental--not
primary--beneficiaries of a tax deduction or credit.) Ac-
cordingly, a federal credit would have to apply to more
than private tuition. A Congress wary of increasing federal deficits might be very reluctant to enact a credit so
broadened.

Why analyze the tuition tax credit if its chances
have so dimmed? For more than a decade those who would
gain have let neither doubts about constitutionality or
political defeats stop their efforts to promote the tuition tax credit. Now that tax subsidization of private-
school tuition is known to be constitutional (provided a
certain legal form is followed), efforts to pass the
credit are bound to intensify. While large federal deficits may be an obstacle to passage of a credit in 1983 or
1984 they will not always be so. Eventually, a serious
effort will be made to enact an education tax credit whose
main intended beneficiaries are those who pay private-
school tuition.[13]

NOTES

1. George H. Gallup, "The Fourteenth Annual Gallup
Poll of the Public's Attitudes toward the Public Schools,"
Phi Delta Kappan, 64(1):   39.
2. Current Population Reports (U.S. Bureau of the
Census), Series P-23, no. 121, *Private School Enrollment,
Tuition and Enrollment Trends: October 1979* (1982), Table 1.
3. Gallup, 39.
4. Current Population Reports, 3.
5. Current Population Reports, 3, Table B.
6. The gains in the South may reflect efforts of
whites to avoid the process of desegregation of public
schools. See statement by Arthur S. Fleming, Chairman,
U.S. Civil Rights Commission, in *Tax Exempt Status of Pri-*

vate Schools, hearings of a subcommittee of the House Ways and Means Committee (1979), 730-738.

    7.   Current Population Reports, Table 5.

    8.   Using a median tuition in the South of $738 in 1979, a 50 percent credit for an extra million students would direct an extra $369 million to the South. A half million students in the Northeast would give up a credit worth half a median tuition of $415; and a half-million students in the North Central region would give up a credit worth half a median tuition of $362. The federal government would lose $194 million less in the two regions of the North. The net effect is a loss of $175 million per year. The use of 1979 tuition figures, of course, tends to bias the estimate down.

    9.   Gary Orfield, *Must We Bus?* (Washington, D. C.: Brookings, 1978), 62.

    10.   Orfield, 62, 417. See also, U.S. Commission on Civil Rights, *Desegregation of the Nation's Public Schools: A Status Report* (1979), Table 1, 20.

    11.   National Education Association, Statement on S.2673, The Educational Opportunity and Equity Act of 1982, mimeogr. (July 16, 1982).

    12.   *Christian Science Monitor*, Nov. 5, 1982.

    13.   Although the main intended beneficiaries of a credit bill written in conformity with the 1983 Supreme Court decision would be private-school users, the outcome may be different. The decision makes it mandatory that fees and charges paid to public schools be eligible for any credit. This gives public-school districts the opportunity of imposing a whole array of new fees and charges in the knowledge that half of the cost can be shifted to the federal government. While public-school parents might resist having to pay half of the new fees and charges, non-parent voters might well succeed in pressing districts to shift as many costs as possible to the federal government in this manner. Even parents, who would pay more while their children were enrolled, would benefit in the long run from the reduction of local taxes. Given the large number of public-school students, the revenue loss of an education tax credit written in conformity with the 1983 decision might be some multiple of the estimates of chapter 3. Undoubtedly, such a credit would produce a battle of wits between Congress and local school boards--one attempting to limit access to the federal benefit, the other to gain greater access.

INDEX

Tuition Tax Credits for Private Education

AN ECONOMIC ANALYSIS

UNTIL NOW advocates and opponents of the tuition tax credit—alo
with other analysts—have asked important questions about the like
effects of a tax credit.

This book provides for the first time statistical estimates of the k
economic relationships that allow analysts to clarify the likely effects
a tuition tax credit.

The answers that emerge suggest that the tuition tax credit m
well be more costly than expected, run counter to federal policies
public school desegregation, and help beneficiary groups only in
inefficient manner.

DONALD E. FREY is associate professor of e
nomics at Wake Forest University, Winston-Sale
North Carolina.

He is a graduate of Wesleyan Universi
Middleton, Connecticut, and of Princeton Univ
sity, Princeton, New Jersey, where he received
doctoral degree in 1972.

He is a member of The Southern Econor
Association. His articles on the economics of e
cation have appeared in such journals as *Jour
of Education Finance, Economics of Education i
view, Public Finance Quarterly,* and *Journal of i
man Resources.*

IOWA STATE UNIVERSITY PRESS • AMES, IOWA 500

ISBN: 0-8138-1826